Fueled by
Coffee and Love

real stories by real teachers

edited by Mari Venturino

For anyone who calls themselves Teacher,
your story matters.

♡ Mari Venturino

P.S. Remember to thank
a teacher!

Table of Contents

Foreword

Dear readers, teachers, and leaders,

This book is for you.

It was made with you in mind, and it was made in your honor.

Before I started this project, I bought into the lie that "I'm only a teacher, what difference can I make beyond my 120 students?" I compared myself to all the administrators, TOSAs, and district-level administrators making a big impact. There are also the EduCelebrities--the ones doing amazing things in their classrooms and sharing about it on social media (although, look deeper, and most aren't even classroom teachers anymore). Yeah, that's not me.

One day, back in February 2017, it hit me. It's not about being an EduHero, it's about being authentically me. I wake up every morning to face the joys and challenges in my middle school classroom. Some days I feel like the fun teacher I always imagined I'd be, and some days I'm weighted down with disappointment or frustration. This is the reality of teaching. Every day. We pour our hearts into these young lives, hoping that we get it right and make an impact.

My 8th grade AVID students were doing 20Time Projects, and I decided to jump in and do one alongside them. In true passion project fashion, this ignited my desire to highlight and amplify the voices of the teachers around me.

So, this is my Daring Greatly moment (if you haven't already, I highly recommend you read at least one of Brené Brown's books!): I have compiled 53 stories from teachers all across the world. These are our stories, and these are your stories. These are not Hollywood stories, or stories by EduCelebrities-- these are stories by people who consider themselves to be "just a teacher," but really are so much more.

Grab your cup of coffee, find your favorite reading spot, snuggle up to your dog or cat or human companion, and enjoy!

Love,
Mari

Introduction

I'm going to say something that would be controversial in the current education sphere, but I want you to bear with me. Whatever you do, don't read what I'm about to say and close this book in disgust and horror, tossing it across the room and making a face like you've stepped in something the dog did. Breathe, and stay with me. Contain your shock. Don't cry out. In the parlance of my students, who know I'm "hip" and "with it" because I use words like parlance to describe lingo, and words like lingo to describe slang- Don't @ me, bro.

Ready? Ok. *deep breath*

I like to learn through lecture.

...

Still there? Still with me? Good. (By the way, isn't an extended article or blog basically a lecture? It's one person talking at readers who don't have a chance to respond in the moment...huh.) More specifically than lecture, I like to learn through stories. It's one of my favorite ways to learn something- to sit with someone who knows some things over a coffee and swap tales. My earliest favorite teachers were all storytellers.

When I was in high school I was a lifeguard. I talk about this a lot, but it's because those were formative times. The Yoda of the guards was a man named Brian Yepp. Brian had been a lifeguard so long he gave Jesus a swim test before allowing Him to make His walk across the waves. Brian taught all of us about lifeguarding, but he did all of it through stories. He wouldn't just tell us we needed to train to be a team as hard as we did and that we should push each other so hard, he'd tell us about the time he was a beach guard and he had to perform a spinal rescue on a skimboarder who'd t-boned into the sand head-first, and how he knew he was up on all his skills but when he looked across that spine board he saw someone he knew wasn't and how that felt. He'd tell us about the time he was nearly drowned by a victim because he was overconfident when he went in. He'd tell us about leaders he knew and how they'd led. And that echoed down through the ranks. Those who came after him found their own stories, everyone has them if you know where to look. The culture of the pools was born in stories, and it was through stories that we all learned.

In college I was an ok student. I excelled in the classes I cared about, and did well enough in the classes I didn't. I was strongest in my theater classes (which are all about forms of storytelling), and my education classes. Not so much the early ones, full of theories, but the later ones where the professors were trying to take education students and turn us into educators. The difference was storytelling. We'd ask a question in class and the professor wouldn't turn to the book, she or he would get a look and say, "Well, when I was teaching fifth grade for twenty years I actually saw that and..." That's instructive in a way a theory can never be.

It's not groundbreaking to say that experience is the best teacher, but that really only works internally. My experiences are my best teachers. Until I learn to communicate them outwards in a relatable way. At that point they can become teachers for anyone who cares to listen.

Think about any education conference you've been to. What presenter resonates the best with you- the one who tells you about this awesome new product she knows all about and how you can use it in your class, or the one who has been using the thing in her own class? Who's got the better stories? Whose stories are better teachers?

But what are the best parts of conferences? It's not the sessions, it's the hallways. It's meeting other teachers and talking shop in a way that we can never do with Normal People. Normal People don't get it, maaaaan. You weren't there, you don't know. Sure, your friends will politely nod and smile along with your hilarious story of a lesson gone awry, but you both know they're praying for a phone call, a text, violent illness, a fire, locusts, anything to give them a way out. They don't even know. But other teachers, we get it. We know.

And in all those interactions, in all those stories, there's learning. That's the thing about stories from teachers, they're authentic. You can't fake it. Why do you think there's been exactly one good TV show about a school in the history of television, and it needed Gabe Kaplan and John Travolta? Non-teachers always get it wrong. And the audience senses it.

Unless they're politicians or selling something. Then, for some reason, people think the truth is out there. When it comes to education policy the public will listen to men and women who have never stood in front of a classroom, who have no idea what students are actually like, what the job is actually like, what we're actually like, and the likelihood of bears. They think since they went to school they know the score. Just like because I've watched a movie I can tell Tarantino where to put the camera.

So why do they get away with it? Because most teachers are too busy doing the work to tell the stories of the work. Because teaching is a job than changes every single day and even the best of us are always running to keep up. It's hard to tell the story as you're living it.

Which is why this book and books like this are so important. Yes, it's a valuable tool for other teachers, we can read and learn from each other. We see ourselves, our classrooms, our students reflected in these pages. We see the truth. But we need Them to see it too. Those who aren't in the classroom, parents, friends, politicians, that guy on Facebook who constantly posts about how easy greedy teachers have it. These stories need to be for them too. Sure, they can still turn a blind eye, but it's harder to do when the bright light of, "No, I've been there, I live this, look," shines.

Life is a classroom. Experiences are teachers. Stories are lessons. Education is for everyone.

Doug Robertson, *5th grade teacher*
Oregon
May 2017

Why I Teach

If you think in terms of a year, plant a seed; if in terms of ten years, plant trees; if in terms of 100 years, teach the people.

-Confucius

What I Remember Most

Samantha Lovett

As adults, many of us remember some of the teachers we had growing up. In some cases, we remember the teachers who made us feel special or valued. In others, we remember those who gave us a hard time. I remember being asked to read aloud Stellaluna to my first grade peers on a day when my teacher was feeling sick. I have memories of my second grade teacher and her obsession with bears and how when she broke her leg, I helped her heat up her microwaveable meals. It's funny what we remember. My third grade year, though, stands out to me most.

Third grade was a transition year for me. I was the new girl in class. I had recently transferred into the accelerated program at another school which meant leaving my close friends and all that was familiar to me behind. The students in my third grade class had been in school together for a few years already. Friendships were already established. This can be intimidating, especially as a young child. The students, though, welcomed me into their group and I quickly became close friends with a few of the girls in class. Coincidentally, I ended up teaching with one of them in Chicago Public Schools when I first began my career.

One of the reasons why I feel I was so quickly accepted was because the classroom community was set up for this kind of thing. Everyone belonged and had a place there. I thank Mr. R for his hard work in making that the norm. The classroom felt like a home away from home. That's what every student should want, right? I know that in my own classroom, I want the students to feel like it's their second home as well. Each morning, as my second graders are filing into the classroom, I give them a greeting. They initiate the greeting and get to choose either a hug, handshake, high five, or fist bump. I'm one of those lucky teachers who receives many hugs! We also start the day with a morning meeting on the rug. The students give a handshake and greeting to their neighbors, they share out any news in their lives, and then we discuss any important announcements.

When I think back to my time in third grade with Mr. R and the other students, there are a few things that I remember most. One of them was story time. Even now, close to 20 years later, I vividly remember this part of the day. We would gather on the rug together and quietly take in the lessons of the stories we read. Mr. R read us books that helped us learn from others. The Man Who Loved Clowns by June Rae Wood was one book I remember. It's a story about a family who has a son with Down's Syndrome and how the family learns from him and his needs. Mr. R also read us The Last of the Really Great Whangdoodles by Julie Andrews. This book follows the journey of Melinda, Thomas, and Benjamin Potter who travel to a mystical place called Whangdoodleland with the help of their friend and mentor Professor Savant. I am currently in the middle of reading this to my own class.

I also remember the project-based learning from third grade. One science project we did was building and launching rockets. After taking the time to build our rockets and adjusting and designing them to our specifications, it was launch day. I remember the sun was shining extra bright. We waited patiently until it was our turn at the launch pad, our palms growing sweaty in the hopes that our rockets wouldn't embarrass us with failing to lift off. The energy (and heat!) of the blacktop was palpable as

Mr. R shot off each rocket one at a time. It was such an exhilarating experience to see the end result of what it was we had worked so hard on.

A second project I fondly remember was having the opportunity to be pen pals with a musher from the annual Iditarod race in Alaska. The Iditarod takes place each year in March. Mushers and their teams of loyal sled dogs make the journey through Alaska until they reach the finish line in Nome. During the 1998 race, each of us received a pen pal and we took time learning about the Iditarod and writing letters back and forth with our mushers. I remember my musher's name was Charlie and he looked like a thinner version of Santa Claus. Charlie sent me a pair of used dog booties from the race, dog smell still intact, and I felt extremely important to receive something so authentic.

In all of these memories, I don't remember the standards that were being taught or what formative assessments were given leading up to the culminating projects. I don't remember weeks of test-prep leading up to a standardized test that may have pushed some of us to anxiety. I remember the experiences Mr. R provided for me and how those experiences made me feel. I try to take what I remember from that year and apply it in my own classroom.

As educators, it's important to be aware of the fact that while we may stress about meeting all the standards in a year's time or worry about how the students' test scores affect our evaluations, the students themselves will not remember those things. They will remember their home away from home, they will remember how they felt valued and a part of a community, and they will remember all of the things their teachers helped them experience.

About Samantha Lovett

Originally from a small rural town in northern Illinois, Samantha moved to Chicago for college and began her teaching career in Chicago Public Schools. She is now teaching second grade in a Des Plaines public elementary school. Her seven- and eight-year-old students keep her laughing and on her toes at all times. Samantha currently lives in the city with her boyfriend and puppy Lydia. When she is not teaching, she likes to explore new restaurants, do crossword puzzles, and spend time with her family and friends.

From Hotel Lobbies to the Classroom

Giulia Longo

I love seeing the look on parent's faces at Back to School night when I tell them that my undergraduate degree is in Hotel Management (technically, Parks, Recreation, and Tourism with an emphasis in Hotel Management). It's a combination of a look of shock and puzzlement. Then, without fail, a look around the classroom.

"Huh," they must think. "How did she go from hotel management to teaching?"

Yup. I went into college thinking if I had a hotel management degree, I would work in glamorous hotels and travel the world. I could not have been more wrong. Working in a hotel was great. For the first month. Then, I got tired of the people guests constantly complaining, overbooking the hotel, and no vacation (let's be real, I teach because I love it and the students, but I also like the vacation). My two days off a week were Tuesday and Wednesday. I needed to do something to keep from going crazy sitting at home. There was an elementary school right by where I lived and I knew that they probably needed volunteers. I looked into it and signed up to be a volunteer during my days off.

I was spending my entire day off helping in either a kindergarten, first grade, or second grade classroom. I would get home after having volunteered and be so happy. I was doing something that meant something. Students would see me walking around the neighborhood and come up and say hi. The pride and joy I felt was unbelievable. I knew that I needed to get myself into a classroom, but this time as a teacher.

I looked into programs and found one that worked best for me - University of Southern California's Masters of Arts in Teaching Program (MAT@USC) online - applied, and was accepted.

Then came the work. One and a half years of being in a classroom bell to bell volunteering, student-teaching, and learning. I was living in Utah at the time and found work in a school relatively close to home. I was going to be working in a kindergarten classroom for the first few months. It's important to note that I went into teaching convinced that I would be a kindergarten teacher. That was my dream - to teach little children how to read and write. It's also important to note that while I consider myself a warm and fuzzy person, I have a very, how shall I put it, big personality. I'm a bit too much for kindergarten. Nevertheless, here I was in a kindergarten classroom. I would be observing and volunteering in this classroom for about 5 months. I learned so much in these 5 months. The teacher I was placed with was a brand new teacher who had (and still has) amazing ideas. She was so passionate about what she was doing and transferred her love of teaching to me. I loved going in each day and working with her. I learned what it was like to be a teacher with her. The biggest lessons I learned were that you need to take care of yourself before you can take care of the kiddos, that if centers aren't working it's ok to stop midway through and change, and how to communicate with parents effectively. But most importantly, I was beginning to develop my own teaching style.

It was then time to start my actual student teaching. For this, I decided to start in fourth grade. I was still convinced I wanted to teach kindergarten, so if I started in fourth grade and got the upper grade student teaching done, it'd be better. The same school I had been in had a fourth grade teacher willing to take me on and she was amazing. Much of what I did when I was given my very own classroom was modeled after what I learned from her. I went into fourth grade knowing that I loved kindergarten more. Then, I taught fourth. What an amazing grade to teach! What an amazing age! The curriculum is my favorite - math is fun because you are getting into the more complex concepts, reading is even more fun because you can read quality books that are longer than 10 pages, and the science is taken to another level and is just cool. I was learning so much about what I wanted to be like as a teacher, I couldn't take notes fast enough. I was itching to get into my own classroom, but still had another semester of school to finish.

From Salt Lake City, I did another ten weeks of student teaching in a K/1 combo classroom in San Diego. That was a valuable experience in that I learned what I knew I didn't want to be like as a teacher. Still valuable, just in a different light. Looking back, those ten weeks were important. They taught me how to work with people that I do not see eye to eye with and how to bring forth new ideas in an environment that may be resistant to change. Those ten weeks also taught me more about myself as a teacher, how to seek out others that have similar thoughts and ideas, and the importance of seeking out those peers. Finally, I learned that as much fun as kindergarten is, boy is it hard work. Did I still want to teach kindergarten or did I want to teach upper grades? I thought about this for a while and then realized, while I would be happy teaching any grade, I would be the happiest in an upper (3rd-5th) grade.

I was hired pretty quickly after finishing my program and taught in a private school for two years. I lucked out and was hired to teach fourth grade. I had the freedom to structure my classroom how I wanted and it was during this time that I truly began to develop and better my practice. I sought out opportunities to collaborate with teachers from around the United States and the world. I continued to be on the lookout for best practices to implement in my classroom. I reflected daily on my practice and made adjustments based on the needs of my students. I was a teacher. The first day of school, I remember standing in front and welcoming the my students, their eager eyes looking at me and me looking at them.

In my mind, all I could think was, "Holy cow, I'm a teacher. Whether they learn or not is all up to me. We better get started." And the rest, as they say, is history.

About Giulia Longo

Giulia is a fourth grade teacher in Chula Vista (San Diego), California. She is in her fourth year of teaching and third year teaching fourth grade. She has had a variety of educational experiences from Montessori to public to private schools and has taken the positives from each to weave into her own practice. She is the co-founder of EdCamp Chula Vista. You can find her on Twitter @mslongo123 or @EdCampCVESD.

My Students Saved Me

Kat Ling

The year I turned 30, I found out that I had cervical cancer. I ended up having surgery after surgery for about a year, and the doctors finally told me that the cancer was gone. Fast forward to a year later, the cancer was back, worse than ever. I was told that I had two choices; either have a hysterectomy or die. It seemed crazy at the time because I couldn't imagine not being able to have kids of my own. I had planned my whole life around having kids someday; to not have any was unimaginable.

The class I had at the time was amazing. They definitely saved my life. I was so depressed after the surgery that I could barely function. I would burst into tears over nothing. My class started inviting me to their stuff.

"Hey, Miss Ling, want to come to my soccer game this weekend?"

"Miss Ling, we have a hockey game tonight, it would be nice if you came to see us play."

At the time, the last thing I felt like doing was going to a game or even going out at all. All I wanted to do was sit home and cry, but I went to those games. I became really close with one family during that time. Their mom was amazing to me. "You can be their second mom. I will share them with you," she said to me. At the time, this made me cry. Everything made me cry. However, this was exactly what I needed to hear. I can remember one time, I had been away for a check-up and the next day her son asked how it had gone. I said it had been pretty awful.

"Why didn't you call us?" he asked, meaning his family. It was so sweet to think that this 12- year old had such empathy for someone who wasn't even part of his immediate family, and it was then that I realized how lucky I was.

Over the year, those students became "my kids" and they were such a special group. They were able to make me smile even when I did not feel like smiling. They were so silly and it was exactly what I needed.

I can remember rolling my eyes at one of them one time. He asked me, "How do you do that?" He then tried to copy me, but he was rolling his whole head. How can you not smile at that? He would do other silly things too. Every now and again, he would come up to me and say in this silly voice, "No you go, no I go, no we both go", then he would sit down and I was left shaking my head, smiling. He was one of the students inviting me to soccer on a weekly basis. Their team got to know me quite well over the next few years and they even gave me a trophy for best fan and insisted I come to the end of year party. To say that our school community sort of absorbs you into their families is putting it mildly.

There were so many times that made me laugh over the course of that year. Eventually I stopped feeling so sad. I started looking forward to their games, sitting with their parents, and cheering them on. It didn't feel so horrible anymore to not be able to have kids because I began to realize that I had a whole classful of kids that I cared about.

Probably the sweetest thing that happened though, and one that will forever touch my heart, was what happened the next year. All of these kids had moved on to high school and while they still stopped in to visit occasionally, they would come a couple at a time, never in large groups.

On October 29, 2010, I got a visit after school from almost my entire class from the previous year. I was shocked and surprised to see so many of them all together, especially since some were not in the same friend circles. They said they came that day because they knew it was the anniversary of my surgery and they wanted to make sure I was okay.

I am still blown away by this gesture and show of caring by probably over three quarters of my previous class. Anyone who knows 13-year olds knows that they sometimes get caught up in their own stuff and are too busy to notice what is going on around them. So for one of them to remember, and organize that they would all come back on this day, still brings tears to my eyes when I think of it. I actually get a bit choked up even writing this because it touches my heart so much.

I truly believe that I was given this class to help me through this difficult time in my life. I honestly wouldn't have made it through it without them. At some points I actually believed that it would be easier to just not be alive, but their inviting me to their games made all the difference. It's sometimes the simplest things that can make the biggest difference for someone. That year was a huge year of learning for me; as those kids taught me so much about empathy for others.

I am still in touch with a lot of these kids and their families. They are adults now and it's so strange to see how they have changed and grown over the years. I still look back on this crazy class and smile. One of them messaged me the other day asking for the web address for our blog; she wanted to look back and do some reminiscing. It's nice to know they liked our class as much as I did. I know I will always look back on this class and smile.

About Kat Ling

I have been teaching in Surrey for the past 12 years; this is my 10th year at my school. I feel so blessed to get to work with such a great group of kids. I want to do everything I can to help them develop and utilize their strengths so they can be successful in the future. Learning is a passion of mine and I am so lucky I can share my love of learning with my students and hopefully foster a love of learning in them.

Who Knew? (I Should Have!)

Mary-Lou Dunnigan

The simple truth to my 30 years in education was that everything I ever wanted to know about teaching was always right in front of me in my students. I'm so glad I listened, observed, documented and responded. You can't help but be transformed and inspired when you learn alongside learners.

I find myself thinking about 'school' more times than I thought I would. Don't get me wrong, retirement is the best kept secret between retirees yet, when your days which for years, were ruled by September starts, daily bells, endless unit plans, curriculum binders, reporting periods and designated vacations, this new life seems a bit odd for the first while. Perhaps this happens to everyone when they retire from their place of work, but I wonder if for educators when we leave, if a little piece of us remains forever with school. I'm slowly convincing myself that this oddness is normal and when I do feel a little 'school sick' as I call it, I pull out a box of keepsakes curated over the past 30 years which remind me of the heart to heart connections created with kids in classrooms that became our homes for the months we were together. People on the outside of education may have an understanding that an educator with a 30 year career would have influenced many students, but I know differently from living it; I was the one privileged to be influenced, or perhaps more accurately, impacted by students. So goes my story of "Why I Teach" which took place at St. Bernard Catholic School with a very special 28...

A few years ago, I taught a great group of grade 5 students. We started our year together reading Katherine Paterson's classic novel, "Bridge to Terabithia." The story took us on a compelling journey together through the highs and (very) lows of two best friends Jesse Oliver Arrons, Jr. and Leslie Burke. The book cover tells the reader that the friendship developed between Leslie and Jess, and the worlds of imagination and learning that she opens up to him, change him forever and enable him to cope with the unexpected tragedy that touches them all. (Spoiler Alert! Leslie dies after falling from a tree that leads over to their secret world called Terabithia.) The story is nuanced by Jess' relationship with his little sister May Belle, who begins to feel a little left out when her big brother, whom she worships, begins to spend time with his new friend Leslie. When Christmas time approaches, Jess saves up his money to buy a Barbie Doll for his little sister because 'somehow this year May Belle needed something special.'

In the spring of the previous year, my father was diagnosed with terminal cancer. At the beginning of the following December he went into palliative care, and I made the decision to take a leave from school to be with my parents. My grade fives weren't aware of why I was leaving, and I was blessed that a teacher who had recently retired from the school came into sub which made for an easy transition for all. I knew the kids would be well taken care of with Mrs. Rock and December for them would be that magical time of the year. Dad passed away in late December. It was a very difficult time. I wasn't sure what returning to school in January would be like. Mrs. Rock had shared the news with my kids, who did what kids do best, sent handmade cards that made you laugh and cry at the same time.

I headed back to school after Christmas holidays feeling anxious and still somewhat emotionally exhausted, but hopeful that school routines would be good. The kids greeted me at the entrance door, hugs all around, sharing stories of what I had missed in December. We gathered at carpet- the space which I deemed to be the most intimate in our classroom. This was the carpet where we visualized Jesse losing to Leslie in the first running race of the school year, the carpet where we sadly uncovered that Jesse had a difficult time at home, the carpet where our minds created a vision of Terabithia where Leslie spoke, "O Spirits of the Grove", the carpet where the candle that represented Les' life was blown out on the same day when Jesse had spent the perfect day with Miss Edmunds. As we gathered that January day on the carpet, sharing stories and becoming reacquainted, a small package wrapped in Christmas paper was handed to me by one of the kids with the accompanying words, "Ms Dunnigan, we knew you needed something special this Christmas." (Terabithia at its finest. I'm certain Katherine Paterson would agree.)

Inside the box was the most beautiful crystal ornament which collectively the kids had decided would be the best reminder of my dad. In that moment, my head buzzing, and tears flowing, I realized that this very special group of fivers got 'it'; an understanding of empathy and compassion- the whole gamut of what can be love on many levels. Who knew? (I should have!) I wanted to believe, and I do, that the Terabithian experience which we 'lived' together on carpet for three weeks at the beginning of the school year, had made us a family, a unit who were connected by words written by Katherine Paterson.

To this day, when I page through my copy of Bridge to Terabithia, I see the scribbled notes in the margins where we just had to stop for a chat, or to catch our breath, or yes, to cry (even if some of us tried to hide our faces behind our novels). More importantly though, when I run my fingers through those pages, I think of those 28 kids, who on that January day, lifted me up and changed my heart forever. Who Knew? They knew! And that is why I taught for 30 years and why I think of school more times than I thought I would.

About Mary-Lou Dunnigan

Mary-Lou has recently retired from a 30 year career in education. She always believed that the questions she had about education could be answered by those sitting in front of her. Student voice, agency and advocacy had been always at the forefront of her actions, whether it be working alongside students, teachers, preservice candidates, parents or administration. She now observes the educational transformation from the sidelines.

Learning from Trouble

Brian David

We all have that one student.

The one who frustrates us beyond belief. The one who makes grey hair grow prematurely or, in my case, fall out. The one that keeps us up at night. But, some of them also remind us as to why we became a teacher.

The first student to do this to me was James during my second year of teaching.*

I have had nightmares of James. He was the student trying to undermine literally everything I ever did in the classroom. He was the one who didn't care about anything. The one who was only here because of his parents. He would put his head down, throw things, and make the weirdest noises to just get the attention of others. He's the one I would be snarky with after his condescending remarks towards others, including me. He was the one I wanted to give up on. But, he was also the one who needed to be here.

According to James, his parents would not let him transfer to a different school.

James' parents put him in a Catholic high school because they were worried what would occur if he would wind up at the local public high school in East LA. That school has a 35% graduation rate and one that is much lower for young men. His parents sent him to my school: one of three predominantly lower income male Catholic schools in Los Angeles. His parents thought by attending here, the small classroom environment would force him to change. They could barely afford the minimum tuition of $100 a month, but they made it work.

So, the first day of his junior year, James walked into my class and told me he's going to fail. I was shocked, but did my best to give James every opportunity not to.

Unfortunately, James failed my class twice. He 'earned' two F's throughout my two semesters of teaching junior English. I played 'bad cop', 'good cop', 'interrogator', 'supporter', 'friend', 'big brother', and 'tough guy'. He never turned in a paper even though he would have notes, would never turn in a project even though he looked at the expectations, and would never participate in a Socratic Seminar even though he knew the topic. After over a year of teaching James, I, along with several teachers, had zero results with him. I did not understand James. I thought I tried everything, but I still couldn't get James to contribute to the class.

The simple answer is that I was wrong. It took me James to realize that. He burst my ideological bubble and made me a better teacher.

Because of James, I realized there are things occurring in my students' lives, which I can never imagine. For James, in between his junior and senior summer, his brother was murdered in front of him. It was then that I realized my expectations were not important. There is so many more important aspects of 'schooling', which I was failing to teach.

It took me this event to realize that some students are at school to escape life around them. For these students, school is a safe zone and a place where they are protected. While I always push for academic progress and achievement, I've matured in how I push students. Reflecting now, I was the most incredibly selfish person compared to the lives our children face every day. I cared more about how my students performed on tests and projects than the journey itself.

James changed my teaching. I took him out to lunch after an awful day of summer school. He told me the realistic expectations he had because everybody knew he wasn't 'smart'. He knew the life he was going to live even though his parents wanted something else.

I wouldn't be the same teacher without James. He taught me to open up my heart and truly feel for my students. A teacher has to listen and not judge. Sometimes, listening is the greatest part of being a teacher.

The reality is that we can all complain about a "James", but my challenge is what can we do to make him or her succeed. Success is different for all students and doesn't occur solely on a state test. Being a teacher is one of the most gratifying professions out there, but there are definitely highs and lows. However, it is up to us to grow as professionals by listening to some of our toughest students.

*All names have been changed

About Brian David

Brian David is an English Teacher at Cathedral High School in Downtown Los Angeles. He teaches a variety of grades and loves hiking, reading, and a solid round of golf. Outside of the classroom, he can be found enjoying the beautiful beaches of Southern California with a novel in his hand.

An Unknown Impact

Jessica Koch

From the first time I enrolled as a student majoring in education, I can remember my instructors asking me why I chose to be a teacher. After changing my major to education from a more lucrative and creative career choice, I often pondered this very question. In college and even after becoming a teacher, I often questioned why I chose to change my major to something that would pay me less and receive very little admiration from others. Was I crazy? Or was there something else beyond what I could comprehend? Was I being "called" into teaching so that God could use me at just the right moment for just the right student? Needless to say, sometimes we all have questions that we think we will never know the answers to.

After completing my student teaching in New Zealand and beginning my first teaching assignment in Tennessee, I always felt like I was a different teacher because I refused to give up on my students by sending them out of my classroom. I was not afraid to contact parents and guardians in hopes that we would support each other through the ups and downs of their child's middle school career. I loved doing what we in education call cross-curricular teaching- meaning if I was teaching math, it would not be unusual to see my students writing, reading, or learning about geography. Within the first two years of teaching, I had this feeling that I was exactly where I was supposed to be career-wise, but no matter what I found myself sponsoring, teaching, coaching, or engaging in, I still found myself wondering why I chose to be a teacher?

Throughout my days in the public education classroom, I have had students who have come across my path who are unforgettable. Some were spunky, some were needy, some were outgoing, and some excelled. I wish that, as a teacher, I could say that I never forget a face or name, but unfortunately, that is not true. With over a thousand names and faces rolling around in my head, what once was a seemingly easy task- remembering names and faces- has now become pretty tough. With each student who entered my classroom, I would wonder about the impact I had made, if any, on their life or educational journey.

In 2010 after seven years of teaching, I was approached by a seventh grade student who was in my fifth period English classroom. He wanted to skip physical education to talk about life. Actually he wanted to talk about something more serious. He wanted to speak with me so he could learn about my experiences from losing my mom when I was fifteen. During our conversation, this student asked me about my mom's final hours, my regrets, and what life was like after my mom's passing. Looking back now, I cannot remember who did more talking- me or my student- but what I do remember is what happened after the conversation.

Within that week my student's father passed after fighting a courageous nine year battle with cancer. Five minutes past nine and the passing of my student's father, my student called to say he was brave enough to do the things that I was not brave enough to do when my mom was in her final hours. He sat with his father and held his hand until his father's final breath. Before the week ended, this quiet seventh grade boy faced a church packed full of friends, family members, and community members who attended his father's funeral and gave one of the most inspiring eulogies I have ever heard. There was not a dry eye in the over-packed church overlooking the elementary, middle, and high schools in the area. In my heart I cannot help but wonder if our conversation helped inspire him to make it through life's challenges that he faced that week. It was from this conversation and the experiences of that week that I realized I did not chose teaching- it chose me.

Whether you find yourself believing in a higher calling or a greater purpose, I believe that everything happens for a reason. Since my mom's passing when I was in ninth grade, I have had adults all around me reinforce the idea that I was a natural teacher. Personally, I do not feel as though I am a natural teacher, but instead I believe that I am a natural communicator who connects with my students, parents, guardians, and colleagues. No matter where my journey has taken me or what I have been involved in, the stories I will always hold near and dear to my heart are the ones in which I have made a lasting impact on a student.

About Jessica Koch

Jessica Koch, formerly Miss Jordan, Mrs. Warner, or Dr. J, has been teaching in public schools in Tennessee, Georgia, and Oklahoma since 2003. She has taught everyone from three year olds to Vietnam Veterans and everything from fine motor skills to educational leadership graduate courses. Ultimately, she is a lifelong learner who cares about the growth and well-being of others and Auburn football. Currently she can be found at East Central University in Ada, Oklahoma assisting her students with learning about technology that can be used in the classroom and how to become a more effective administrator.

I Love to Learn

Teresa Ozoa

I am a lifelong learner. I teach partly because I want to help my students become lifelong learners, critical thinkers, and contributing citizens, But I teach also because I learn something new every day -- from my students, from what we share -- about literature, about life, about myself.

My juniors gave TED-style talks last spring, through which I learned, among other things, about bats, the history of dance, and Studio Ghibli. During the year I also learned about one student's flight from Syria, another's wins and losses at fencing, and how yet another was coping with the sudden death of his mother.

I have also learned from the 20% Time Projects of students in at least two of my five classes for the past three years, on topics as diverse as 3-D printing, designing kicks, writing a fantasy novel, the history of artillery, and value investing and stoicism. The student who researched the latter read four biographies over the year, including on Marcus Aurelius (the original stoic) and on Warren Buffett (investor extraordinaire), then self-published a 7,000-word guide on Amazon Kindle. Oh, by the way, he also earned a full-ride scholarship to an Ivy League university.

The same goes for my teaching/learning in other contexts. My husband and I are part of our parish RCIA (Rite of Christian Initiation for Adults) team that helps those seeking to become Roman Catholic. Each meeting, the "seekers" inspire me with their thoughtful questions and the challenges of their spiritual journeys, including, at times, acting against the will of their families. And just last week, another teaching team member shared the details of his own beautiful epiphany that stunned us into reflective and respectful silence.

I am continually learning from wonderful/terrible resource called the internet. (At least that's how I justify my avid surfing....) My motto is based in part on Neil Gaiman's 2012 commencement speech in which he told grads at Philadelphia's University of the Arts to "Make Good Art." The transcript became a lovely graphic art book that I like to give to graduates because it applies to all of us, not just artists. I combined this with educator Alice Keeler's admonition to "share what you do to help you reflect on what you do" to form my motto.

The point is to aspire not ONLY to make "great" stuff because one will never be satisfied with it. Even "good" stuff that is sincere and thoughtful and that represents creative work deserves notice. And sharing it helps to make the stuff that follows even better. I hope to encourage my students and colleagues to do the same.

As a young adult I seemed destined to become a perpetual student rather than a teacher and learner. After obtaining a B.A., I stayed on to earn an M.A., a single subject teaching credential in English and a multiple subject credential for teaching elementary school. (All this I accomplished, in typical Stanford fashion, in only four quarters.) After two years teaching at a private high school in Honolulu, during which I spent my summers learning and teaching with the Hawaii Writing Project, I got an itch to go to law school. I earned a J.D., and more important, met my future husband, at UCLA, then worked as a lawyer and legal editor for eight years.

But, when my young family of four moved from northern to southern California, I had to give up the editing job. To figure out my next steps, I followed the process in What Color is Your Parachute? -- a classic job-hunting manual that made me realize I have always been teaching and learning. Even as a legal editor, I coordinated the CLE (Continuing Legal Education) offerings at my office; I volunteered as a religious education teacher for my children's classes; and I took community college courses in programming and knitting (eerily related, as it happens).

The fact that the California legislature had just passed the (now-defunct) class size reduction bill sealed the deal to return to teaching full time, this time with second graders. Eventually, I returned to teaching my first love, literature and writing, at my current high school.

I continued to scratch that deep itch to keep learning by becoming an early adopter of educational technology … which brings me to this group of like-minded educators by way of CUE conferences and Twitter chats, edcamps and tech summits. We share a common love of sharing, of teaching, of learning.

CEO Satya Nadella paraphrased Carol Dweck's observations about education in Mindset to apply to the business world: "Don't be a know-it-all; be a learn-it-all." In an interview with Business Insider, Nadella states, "the 'learn-it-all' always will do better than the other one even if the 'know-it-all' kid starts with much more innate capability…. Going back to business: If that applies to boys and girls at school, I think it also applies to CEOs like me, and entire organizations, like Microsoft." I agree with the learner focus of both Dweck and Nadella.

I ~~LOVE~~ LIVE to learn.

(adapted from July 23, 2014 and August 12, 2014 posts on singsurfknit.wordpress.com)

About Teresa Ozoa

Teresa's current gig at University High School in Irvine CA is teacher of British Lit, rhetoric and writing, although she has also taught 2nd grade GATE and Legal Research and Writing in law school. She was 2015-2016 UHS Teacher of the Year and is a CUE Rock Star Faculty and Lead Learner, Google Certified Educator, EdTechTeam speaker, UCI Writing Project Fellow and speaker, surfer, knitter, reader, writer, sci-fi geek and cosplayer -- able to fix anything with a flashlight, duct tape and Google.

Why I Teach

Jennifer Calderon

My life as a teacher started roughly ten years ago. I was on the verge of graduation from Biola University, and had no prospects of a job in sight. I had discussed my career goals with my professor, and to my surprise he said I would be an excellent teacher. (Well, if I'm being honest, I knew I was meant to be a teacher, ever since I was in third grade. Not to sound sure of myself, but I put my passion on the backburner to pursue a job as a doctor). My dream of being a doctor was thrown out the window when I experienced health issues during my junior year in college.

So here I was a girl with support, passion, and no job. After conversations with my mom, I decided to apply at my alma mater in Hesperia Unified. My interview was perhaps the scariest experience I had ever been through at the time. They asked me questions regarding state standards, teaching strategies and questions I had never even thought about. I knew that only having a Bachelor's Degree in Biology, I was ill prepared for a job in education. I owe it to a past principal and assistant principal for giving me a chance of a lifetime. They offered me a job that same day. Ecstatic, I accepted. Saying "yes" was the best career choice I have ever made.

My first few years were rough. Being fresh out of college and fully immersed in a classroom where finding my pedagogy, defining my classroom management skills and dealing with rowdy students was overwhelming. It wasn't until my second year teaching that I finally felt like I kind of knew what I was doing.

I say all that to bring you here in my story: I've always had a interest in learning. My Mom always tells me the story of being a curious little girl who carried a notepad and pencil behind her ear. This story always makes me smile, because it literally describes my outlook on life. I no longer use a notepad and pencil, but a laptop and my cellphone to discover many facets of the world, and specifically how I can become a more effective teacher in the 21st century.

Learning is something that resonates with me deep to my core. In the years I've been a teacher, I have always had the desire to learn more. Never staying stagnant with teaching strategies and looking for new, fun, and exciting technology in my lessons has always been a driving part of my job. I am so grateful for the passion that was placed in me at such a young age and that has continued to burn presently.

Currently, I am my school site's Team Technology Lead, this position was offered to me three years ago, following the first ever CUE conference I went to. The CUE organization changed my view on education, in my experience I observed the passion that teachers had while incorporating new ideas into their classroom. I was excited about the idea of having technology to explore those ideas with and needless to say, it elevated my interest in how I could do it in my classroom. For three years I've been on a road discovering new technology to incorporate in my classroom, and also to share out with others.

Looking back during the first year as TTL, I was adapting. Life was hard due to this new outlook, but through the experiences with my students and observing their growth, I knew I had to continue. I shared out innovative curriculum ideas with only a few teachers who showed interest. The second year I became more vocal and led some trainings on campus. It was not until the later half of the year that I decided to spread as much knowledge as I possibly could. I began to share out weekly technology tips that allowed me to express my joy, passion and knowledge for technology with my colleagues. My third year, I finally found my groove and niche.

During the summer between my second and third year of being a TTL, I met a remarkable teacher. She and I developed an immediate friendship and bond over technology. I fully feel that it was due to this relationship, that I gained the reassurance and direction I was lacking. It was through our conversations and sharing of knowledge that my purpose as a TTL became clear. From our conversations, I was able to see the value and importance of Twitter for professional development. I felt that by attending national CUE conferences and CUE Rockstars, I was knowledgeable, but didn't know exactly what to do with the information.

Through Twitter chats and following other passionate educators, I gained knowledge of how to display my information. I continued to share my weekly technology tips, but found the confidence to start presenting information not only at my site, but also present at conferences. I applied to one and got rejected. Then, I dusted myself off and applied to another. To my surprise, I was accepted and will present over the summer at CUE Rockstar Chico. For me, this was a huge accomplishment! I have always been comfortable presenting to my students and my peers, because I was in the comfort of my classroom and campus. However, through conversations I have had with my students about building a growth mindset, I had to push past my fixed mindset.

So now, here I am, a teacher who is continually pursuing a profession that allows me to learn. I get to learn new ways to educate other teachers and most importantly my students. The main goal I have is to advocate for all stakeholders to learn 21st Century skills. Whether it be ways for teachers to instruct their students, clerical staff to incorporate more GSuite apps to streamline their workload, or for students to gain necessary skills to equip themselves for the future ahead, I found where I can be used to my fullest potential. Being able to continue to learn, motivate and encourage others is why I teach.

About Jennifer Calderon

Jennifer Calderon is Google for Education Certified Educator and Trainer from Oak Hills, California. She is currently an AP Biology, Honors Biology and Freshmen Focus teacher. Alongside being a teacher she is a Team Technology Leader as well as the ASB Advisor. Jennifer enjoys incorporating G Suite for Education tools to meet the various curriculum standards. She has a passion for teaching students and other educators to become 21st Century learners. In 2013, 2015, and 2017 Jennifer was selected as Teacher of the Year for Oak Hills High School. In 2015, Jennifer was named Secondary Teacher of the Year for Hesperia Unified School District.

Tears

Emily Kath

Tears fall at expected times, like when we experience sadness and tragedy, but there are also many times when tears fall at unexpected times. When I think about my role as a social worker, I recall the first time my tears fell…

I was in my sophomore year of college, taking inorganic chemistry in a lecture hall that easily held 300 students. I struggled to understand the lecture, even though I sat in the very front row in the center of the hall, and I took copious notes every single day; I worked with a tutor in the lab portion of the class and enjoyed seeing chemistry in action. I woke early on a snowy Tuesday morning in early December and trekked across Northern Illinois University's campus, with my head down, focused on arriving to my final exam on time, all the while repeating formulas in my head, so as not to forget them. I sat in the empty hall, wondering where my classmates were, when at 8:07, my professor walked in and said, "Emily, didn't you hear? Exams are cancelled for the day." Tears fell when I trekked back to my dorm room, wondering how this class could be so difficult when my professor, in a class of 300, knew my name. Tears fell as I dreaded the anticipation of taking that final exam an entire week later, when I had been as prepared as I could have been that very day. Tears fell when I wondered what on Earth I was going to do when I failed that final exam and lowered my hard-earned GPA.

I ended up with a D+ in my inorganic chemistry class and immediately decided to explore other career options. Tears fell when I pushed my childhood dream of being a pediatrician to the

46

side. However, a career planning course opened my eyes to the field of social work. I remember shadowing a medical social worker, thinking, "This is it! I need to be a social worker!" It felt so natural, so simple, so wonderful. Tears fell when I realized I had found my calling.

During my undergraduate practicum at a domestic violence and sexual assault center, my tears fell after I responded to the local emergency room for a suspected rape call. Tears fell after I watched countless women return to abusive relationships, anticipating that the women would need our shelter again at some point. Tears fell after I transported children with scabies to the emergency room, and they could simply not get comfortable in their own skin. Tears fell when I graduated with honors and received high regards from my professors. It felt so good to know that I was in the right place. The tears simply fell.

When I first began work after graduate school, I worked with junior high students. These students had real-life problems, and they needed my help to fix them. I enjoyed coaching and sponsoring many activities, seeing firsthand how my job as a social worker impacted students in their social lives. Tears fell when I watched athletes run the cross country course at state. Tears fell when students in the honor society accrued thousands of hours of volunteer service hours. Tears fell when parents thanked me for helping their children succeed.

A few years later, I moved on to work in an elementary school building in a poverty-stricken community. Social work was as real here as it would ever get for me. My tears fell when two of my dearly beloved colleagues died unexpectedly. Oh how the tears fell. When I think of how real, how authentic, how caring these friends were to me and their students, the tears still fall.

Many of my students relied on school for a safe environment and two warm meals; I met the most basic of needs for so many students, and yet, they showed up each and every day to greet me with a smile. Tears fell after a kindergartener disclosed that he was home at the time when a murder took place in his living room. Tears fell after he described the scene that he saw. Tears fell when I determined that the investigating police officers did not report to DCFS that my student and his siblings were present during a murder. More tears fell after I spoke with a DCFS investigator, and he jokingly told me that I ruined his day with my report. Tears fell when this student transferred from our school district to live with his grandmother for the rest of his childhood.

I worked with so many students with extensive familial histories, many of whom were living with extended family members or adoptive parents who they called "mom and dad". So many of my students simply needed someone to love them unconditionally, someone to provide them with structure and rules, someone to cheer for them when all others were cheering elsewhere. Tears fell when I shared an extensive Social Developmental Study on a student being evaluated for special education; I was sharing with the education team the extensive mental health history of his biological mother, the uncertainty of the identity of his biological father, and the likelihood that my student was born under the influence of drugs. It all sounded like too much when I spoke the words aloud. The tears simply fell. Afterward, when I was processing with my Director of Special Education, I apologized for my emotions in the meeting, and Mr. Lambe said with all seriousness, "I was getting a little misty-eyed myself; you did a great job reporting such an extensive history. Besides, I'd never want you to be a Stepford Social Worker." The tears simply fell. I remember the validation I felt when my Director affirmed natural emotions that come from our heart. I remember feeling so grateful to work in a profession where emotions are taught and displayed. More tears fell.

Life as a school social worker is simply an amazing life. To have the ability to explore families and a child's development and to teach the skills necessary for students to have healthy and meaningful relationships just does something to my heart. To have the opportunity to work alongside amazing educators who mold the brains of our children is simply a blessing. Just this year, I moved back to an elementary school in my originating school district, and I have been reminded that tears will continue to fall, for both expected and unexpected reasons, but I have learned over the years to have my Kleenex ready for every last one of them, so the tears will inevitably continue to fall.

About Emily Kath

Emily is in her 10th year of school social work! She is blessed to work at Pioneer Path Grade School in Channahon, IL, with 3rd and 4th grade students and their families!

Teaching in the Balance: Why I Teach

Renee Bogacz

Recently, the high school I graduated from held a career day. They asked alumni of the school to come speak to students about their chosen careers. I briefly considered applying to share with students my experience as a teacher and how I found this career, but I doubted anyone would be very happy to hear what I had to say.

For as long as I can remember, I always wanted to be a teacher. Even as a little girl, I always wanted to play school with my brother and my friends. A woman who was a family friend was a principal and she would often bring me copies of sample workbooks and textbooks or extra copies of worksheets from her school and I would be giddy with excitement at these gifts. Interestingly enough, I also knew very early on that I wanted to be an English teacher. Science and history were interesting, math was a challenge, but reading, writing, and even grammar were so much fun for me! I was an avid book reader and creative writer from the time I could read and write. And if I'm being honest, there's something fascinating to me about grammar and the way our language works. I get enjoyment from creating clarity of ideas from the way words are arranged on a page. So, English language arts teacher was my chosen career path from the very start.

Obviously, language arts class was always my favorite class in school. I was the dork who read every single book and story assigned to me and loved talking about them with people. I was the nerd who loved writing essays and research papers. I was the girl who wrote scores of poems -- most of them lousy, mushy love poems -- as an emotional outlet. I was the person who took meaningful moments in my life and tried to preserve them by writing them as scenes from a story. I was the one who heard a song with exceptional lyrics and thought, "How I wish I had written that song!" or, "I wonder what the backstory is for this song?" I would then proceed to develop a story for the meaning of the song if I couldn't find one through research!

I'm the same way today as an adult. I love reading and discussing books. I love reading and analyzing poetry. I still become mesmerized by beautiful song lyrics. I love doing my own creative writing. I love doing research projects. And I love doing all these things with students as well as teachers, friends, and family. My love of the language, especially in written form, is just part of my fabric. But it took just one single teacher to almost rid me of that fiber.

She was one of my high school English teachers. Mrs. Jackson (not her real name) taught American literature. Since literature classes were always my favorite, I looked forward to this class very much. But it didn't take long to discover that Mrs. Jackson didn't appreciate literature the same way I did.

I can remember three very distinct experiences with her that could have broken me. The first incident came during a class discussion of Nathaniel Hawthorne's story "Young Goodman Brown." Mrs. Jackson was discussing symbolic elements in the story. She talked about the character of Faith and the pink ribbons she wore in her hair. Faith's pink ribbons are traditionally seen as a symbol of her purity or innocence. I raised my hand and asked, "Is it possible that maybe Faith isn't as pure and innocent as she seems? Her ribbons are pink, but isn't white the traditional color of purity? Maybe Hawthorne was trying to show us that

Faith isn't as completely pure as we think she is. That's why he had her wear pink ribbons instead of white."

Mrs. Jackson's response was swift and stinging. "Absolutely not!" she told me. She then went on a rant that sounded something like this: "Her name is Faith. The ribbons are pink, which is a color we associate with innocent little girls. For years and years, experts have explained how her ribbons represent her purity, but you come along as a teenager and think you know this story better than the experts? You don't know anything. I know this story. I'm the teacher. I'm the expert. You need to understand this the way I teach it to you."

Teenager though I was, I can remember thinking, "I don't think that is the way a teacher should tell a student she's wrong. I just had an idea. I just asked a question." It was shocking and a little upsetting, but not demoralizing. Because I was a teenager and prone to being obnoxious, instead of being beaten down by Mrs. Jackson, I preferred to be a pebble in her shoe. I spent that year continuing to ask questions about literature -- sometimes legitimate, sometimes absurd -- just to irritate her.

The "Young Goodman Brown" incident quietly rallied my classmates around me. This was evident in the second distinct incident I remember. It was near the end of the school year, and being the grammar geek that I was, I had finished all the exercises in our grammar workbooks already. Mrs. Jackson had given us a few pages to complete in class. As my classmates worked, I made a little show out of closing my workbook and pulling out a novel to read. Mrs. Jackson glared at me from her podium for ten minutes. When it was time to go over the answers in class, she immediately called on me to read the answers, which I did -- and all correctly, I might add! When I finished, my classmates looked at Mrs. Jackson, who was clearly flabbergasted at not having caught me being lazy or defiant, and they broke out in spontaneous cheers. When they were finally quiet, Mrs. Jackson looked at me and said, "You're not as smart as you think you are, Renee." In my mind at that time, I thought, "Oh, yes, I am!" but later, when I thought about what she had said, I was a bit bothered by the fact that she had basically called me stupid in front of the whole class. She had planted a seed of doubt in my sense of confidence (which fortunately never really took much root).

The final incident came at the end of the school year when it was time to register for next year's classes. Mrs. Jackson refused to recommend me for honors level English, despite having a high B average in her honors level English class and all the honors level English classes previous. She met with my parents and me and told us directly, "Renee doesn't have what it takes to be an honors student." That was the only rationale she offered. And just as an FYI -- my parents fought her recommendation and had me placed in honors English the next year, where I maintained a high B average.

When people ask me why I became a teacher, I tell them I was inspired by Mrs. Jackson, and I share with them my personal experiences as a student in her class. Often, people are taken aback to hear that this is the kind of teacher who inspired me. Mrs. Jackson was not a very good teacher -- it is easy to see this from the three memorable interactions. How could she possibly be inspirational?

I always imagined that there is a big balance scale that all teachers are on: good teachers on one side of the scale, not so good ones on the other side. As long as Mrs. Jackson was teaching, then that scale would always be tipped slightly in favor of the less than desirable teachers. I became completely resolved to even out the balance by being a good teacher.

I vowed to myself never to tell a student he or she is wrong, stupid, or silly for having an idea or asking a question. I vowed to myself never to make a student feel any of those things, either, so I would have to be thoughtful in my language and interactions. I vowed to myself never to play "gotcha" with a student or make a deliberate attempt to humiliate him or her. I vowed to look for reasons to help students achieve their goals rather than find reasons to squash them. I vowed never to let students know who I liked and who I didn't like (because I am only human, after all -- there have been some students I didn't like). I vowed to myself to be the things Mrs. Jackson was not -- open-minded, friendly, helpful, and most of all, kind and unafraid of being vulnerable.

Why do I teach? I teach to keep the scale balanced, and maybe even tipped in favor of the teachers who care more about helping students grow and learn instead of the teachers who care about being right and keeping kids quiet!

About Renee Bogacz

Renee Bogacz has been a teacher for more than 25 years. She transitioned from English language arts to being the instructional technology resource teacher for her district. She has a passion for integrating technology into teaching and learning but keeps her original love for language arts alive by reading and writing about education topics. She recently accomplished one of her long-desired professional goals: becoming a Google Certified Educator. You can follow her on Twitter as she shares professional resources and the exciting things happening in her school district (@mrsbogacz).

I Teach Because She Cared

Ge-Anne Bolhuis

I was six years old when I met her. I thought she was the most beautiful person I had ever seen. She glowed when she smiled and I could tell that she loved children and was really happy that she GOT to teach us! I really wanted her to like me and I worked hard in class. I don't remember ever feeling bored; instead, Miss Coy's class was always fun, engaging, and full of surprises. In the mornings , we started our day with a hearty, if off key, rendition to "Good Morning to You" and our teacher never failed to pushed in and "smush" the dimples on the sides of her face when she sang "we're all in our places...with smiles on our faces...". With Miss Coy, I was safe. And loved.

As first grade progressed, I absolutely adored reading time and one day, after reading all the books in the dishpan buckets, Miss Coy asked me to come with her to the library. First graders weren't allowed to do much in there, except watch filmstrips and remember to be extremely quiet, but on this day, Miss Coy walked me to the back wall where enormous bookshelves towered over my head and told me that I was allowed to pick out a book.

Standing there, reveling in the moment as I tried to choose something would like and was magical and then my eyes rested upon "The Story of My Life" by Hellen Keller. I knew nothing of the author, but somehow the booked title had hooked me. I will never forget how grownup and big I felt when the librarian stamped the due date in that volume--my very first chapter book. I asked Miss Coy why I was allowed to get this treasure and she smiled down at me and said the three words that changed my destiny: "Because you're smart!

After devouring that volume and thousands more as I continued my journey through school and through the school of life, I have always known I wanted to be a teacher--an empowerer and awakener of young people's minds and hearts.

The last day of first grade was a shortened day. We just had to run in and get our report cards and leave. With a quivering lip and holding back crocodile tears, my seven-year old self walked into the classroom where Miss Coy was sitting at a table. She gave me a big hug and her brilliant smile with a gift bag that included a toothbrush and toothpaste. I remember knowing what heartbreak felt like for the first time.

The greatest gift of my first grade year was that, from then on, no matter where I went, though, and no matter what I encountered, I never doubted that I was smart and that I could achieve. Even when things were hard and I was tempted to give up, Miss Coy's voice whispered to me: "You are smart" and somehow I pushed on.

My educational journey through upper elementary school, junior high and high school was atypical, leading me through a fundamental Baptist church-school before my return to the public school arena as a junior. I did well in high school, though as an adult, I clearly see that I could have done better. One fall day in my senior year, around the time of the first frost, we had an assembly. Lots of classmates were dressed up and I wasn't sure why. Though I had spent my junior year back in public school, I was still perplexed by some of the rituals and routines. When the assembly started, I learned that today was the day of National Honor Society (NHS) inductions. Soon, NHS members were stepping down into the audience to inform the new inductees that they had been chosen. I was happy for my classmates and watched with compassion as some were passed by. As I watched one girl swipe away a tear, I felt a tug on my sleeve and realized that my name was being called.

In a dreamlike state, I walked to the stage to receive my yellow rose and certificate and found myself in tears as well as I thought back to that smile and those words: "Because you are smart". A reception followed and at the end of that day, I drove to my old first grade classroom and walked into Mrs. Ray's room (she had married since my time with her). I gave her my rose and thanked her for changing my life.

I entered college the next fall and graduated with a degree in elementary education four years later. I have stayed in touch with Mrs. Ray over the years and watched in amazement as she continued to teach far past the time she could have retired. For over forty years she poured herself into the lives of children and I watched on social media as message after message congratulated her on her retirement and I saw that she had touched scores of lives like she had mine.

It's almost a quarter century since I walked into my first classroom. After three degrees earned along with two additional certification programs, I still hear Miss Coy's voice in my head when I am working on a project, preparing a presentation, or facing a difficult day.

More importantly, because of her example, I know what ability I have to empower others and I understand that I may never know what my positive affirmations might mean to those whom I encounter as I teach, coach, and collaborate.

"Thank you" will never be enough.

About Ge-Anne Bolhuis

Ge-Anne is a high school instructional technology specialist in NW Georgia. She has been an educator for over 22 years and loves building relationships with other educators from all walks of life. She lives with her Dutch husband and two children in Calhoun, Georgia where she can be found engaging in conversations about educational technology, curriculum, and music.

Don't Write Your Notes on Your Arm

Alex Peck

At home I have a t-shirt that my mother-in-law (an amazing educator for over 30 years) gave me one year for my birthday. The t-shirt is a take on the infamous Superman logo and says, "I'm a teacher, what's your superpower?" Many times teachers are compared to superheroes for the work we do and they impact we make in the lives of hundreds of young people's lives every year. Aside from the uplifting and positive similarity is that superheroes and teachers share they also typically both have an origin story. Peter Parker wouldn't have become Spider Man if Uncle Ben hadn't offered his immortal words of wisdom to Peter before his death. Bruce Wayne wouldn't have become Batman if the Waynes just enjoyed a quiet night at the theatre together. As I enter my 9th year of teaching, one aspect of my career that I have always felt self-conscious about is my own origin story as a teacher.

In this line of work, you are blessed to work with some incredible, talented and dedicated teachers. When you put a group of teachers together in a meeting, PD, or any other confined space, the topic will always come back to teaching and why we do what we do each year. Many teachers have uplifting stories about the transformative power of education and how it changed their life and compelled them to enter the field. Others have stories about playing school as young children and waiting for the day that they could do it it in a real classroom. Some teachers come from a pedigree of teachers and were inspired by their grandparents and parents in the family business. I have always struggled in these conversations because I do not have one of the Hallmark moments to share with my colleagues and friends. The reason I chose education is quite simple. My Mom thought I would be good at it. As a Senior in college, I was trying to decide what to do next in life. I could have gone on and pursued a masters related to my degree in political science or I could take a leap of faith and try education. Ultimately I took my Mom's advice and enrolled in the masters of adolescence education program at my undergrad university. The rest as they say is history.

I may not have the greatest story when it comes to why I chose teaching, but the reason why I teach is simple: laughter and joy. If you ask any of the students I have ever had in class they would probably tell you a lot of things about me. One of the top answers though would be that I like to laugh, or more accurately, I like to giggle. So imagine for a second a long haired former football player, wrestler and rugby player that when he starts to laugh doesn't just laugh, he giggles. When I say giggle, I mean like really giggle. Like the kind of giggle that students want to get their phones out and record for posterity. Laughter has and always will be one of the most important aspects of my classroom.

So much so, that in my 2nd or 3rd year I started a list in class. The list is titled: "Don't write your notes on your arm and other things heard in my room." I started the list to remember all of the times that, no matter what the content was we were covering, or no matter how bad someone's day might have been, the whole room was laughing together. I teach because of these moments that students will remember long after they have left my classroom. I teach because hearings kids laughing and enjoying school is just a little bit more important than the Gupta

Empire and their accomplishments. I teach for the moments when I have to lovingly (and a little sarcastically) explain to a student that asking for paper might be a better idea than writing that day's notes on their forearm. The thought process of a teenager can sometimes be puzzling and peculiar. The story which prompted the list demonstrates this. As a 10th grade teacher, you often don't think that you will have to explain to your students that writing their notes on the arm isn't the best decision because studying will be a lot more difficult after a shower.

Every year former students return and ask about the list and share fond memories from their class and their stories that made the list. That is why I teach. Students may not remember what they got on their Regents exam or why the Magna Carta is important, but they will remember the fun times they had in school and how they were treated by their teachers.

The Dalai Lama has said that the best way to have joy in your life is to bring joy to others. I have many years left in my career, but I hope that at the end of it my students can say that they felt laughter and joy in my classroom. With that being said, allow me to share with you the moments that have made my students and I laugh, giggle and enjoy learning history. These are what they consider nowadays "alternative facts". Every quote brings me back to a specific class and student that I have had. My hope is that they bring you laughter and remind you, as the famous Monty Python quote goes, to always look on the bright side of life. But most importantly to remember that it is always best to write down important information on paper and not on a body part.

While discussing the assembly line in Econ:

"Harrison Ford? Didn't he invent the car?"

While discussing Early Humans:

"I wonder what the Neanderthals used their digging sticks for?"

While discussing the American Revolution:

"Do you guys remember Paul Revere?"

"Yeah wasn't he the headless horsemen or was he the guy from the Progressive commercial?

While studying the Cold War: " Wait! Kim Jung Un is a real person? I thought he was just a character from the movies!"

Thoughts on technology:

Student- "Wait! How did people find information before Google existed?"

Me- "Well they used encyclopedias and looked up information"

Students - "What is an encyclopedia and how do you use it?

While discussing the importance of the Age of Exploration:

Me- "What was the most important food to move from the New World to Europe?

Student- "Hot dogs .. definitely hot dogs"

Student Question: "Were the Europeans scared of wooly mammoths when they arrived in the New World?"

Finally sometimes in Global History there can be a lot of different people to remember and sometimes that can get a little tricky ....

"Isaac Newton learned about gravity from Johnny Appleseed. He didn't believe him until he started planting all of those trees."

"What's Hitler's last name?"

"Is Gandhi real?"

"I thought Martin Luther & Martin Luther King Jr were the same person .. They aren't?

"Pearl Harbor is in Boston right?"

Me- "England is a Protestant nation because what fat guy wanted a divorce?

Students - "Santa Claus!?"

"Lenin, he was the guy in the Beatles right? How did he lead a revolution and be in the band?"

I teach because teaching & learning are fun. It's important to not take this crazy thing called teaching too seriously and & to enjoy the precious time we have with our students.

About Alex Peck

Alex is in his 9th year of teaching Social Studies, primarily Global History 10. Alex teaches 10-12 grade at Webster Schroeder High School in Rochester, NY after stops at other great schools along the way. You can usually find Alex poorly impersonating historical figures in my classroom, teaching with pop culture & laughing at his own jokes.

Starring in My Own Epic Adventure

Amanda Houp

I love Epic Adventure Stories. You know, the kind where the most unlikely protagonist is presented with an insurmountable task, and through the unswerving support of a sidekick (or nine), faith in their purpose, and help from the Unseen, they rewrite history with their success. Obviously, Harry Potter, Lord of the Rings, Star Wars, even The Dark Knight series (Hello, Christian Bale), are some of the most popular of our time and I'm just a sucker for these grand, heroic, monumental stories.

Perhaps I love them because complete and utter doom is miraculously avoided. Maybe it is the realm of fantasy that I can escape to. But more likely, it has to do with the sheer humanness of the characters. Humble, unsuspecting, potentially outcasted characters catapult themselves into legend through their sacrifices. Character, fortitude, and loyalty are tested in unpredictable trials. Fragile friendships often shine, even if just barely, in the darkest moments of an era. There are times of hope and hopelessness, pain and healing, tragedy and growth. It's the beautiful (and often ugly) of life on a page.

Don't get me wrong, my life in a small Ozark town is nothing to Frodo's trek through Mordor, Batman's ordeal in the underground prison, or the Battle of Hogwarts.

So, why and how do these stories resonate with me so much? Because despite the contrast in settings and conflicts, I see so much that is necessary to a meaningful life. I am the protagonist of my own adventure. I must choose good and life and sacrifice. I must lead, if not fearlessly, at least faithfully. Many times my success depends on a loyal friend who sees in me something greater than what the mirror reveals. That "there is some good left in this world...and it's worth fighting for" (Tolkien).

My story is about me just trying to fight the good fight and lead others to do the same. My platform is my classroom, the literature I teach, the questions I ask, and the ideas I seek from my students. It's so cool: literature and stories are the perfect place to invite students to not only learn to read, think critically, and write logically, but also an opportunity for personal growth. I challenge students to care--really be passionate--about something or someone; to ask questions and find solutions that can make a difference; to be reflective about their words and actions so they help and not hurt their community.

In every Epic Adventure there is a Mordor. Voldemort. Darth Vader. These nemeses strike fear into the hearts of any hobbit or superfan. The adversaries in my story are apathy, selfishness, and laziness. Whether it be juniors who have given up on school, seniors who refuse to consider their future, kids who don't care about anything but Snapchat, or classrooms that are stuck in 1982, I battle with as much energy and passion that I can. I love showing that the witch hunt of Salem in the 1600s mirrors the political scandals of the last 20 years. That Hamlet was the snarkiest of all young men, and not even these sixteen-year olds could out-sass him. How the "criminals" of Poker Flat are so much more than a gambling, drunken rabble. I love giving them 20 percent of their time to explore something that matters to them, watching them unfold layers of creativity, until even the most shut down, "uninspired" student suddenly wows their peers. Indifference and thoughtlessness are strong foes, but my resilience must be stronger.

And in all these stories, there is a sidekick (or several): Ron and Hermione, Han Solo and Chewy, Grover (Percy Jackson), Horatio. A character who devotes their energy and wit to the struggling protagonist. My favorite sidekick, the one that exemplifies the best qualities of humanity is a plump little hobbit named Samwise Gamgee. You realize, don't you, Frodo would not have made it, Middle Earth would still be under Sauron's control, and Aragorn would be ever high-tailing it across the landscape trying to avoid the Nagul. Sam is a big deal. He carries most of their supplies. He chases off the sneaky little Gollum. He literally carries Frodo up the burning mountain after hundreds of miles of walking. And most importantly, he speaks life, hope, and purpose into Frodo's ear when life, hope, and purpose are being snuffed out. We all need a Samwise. Someone who recognizes the value and greatness in us, even when we can't see it in ourselves. Someone who chases away doubts and helps us learn from our pain. I think a lot of our students need a Sam and I hope for the short time they are in my classroom, they feel the support and encouragement they need to take their next step. My Samwise is my husband, the father of my children, and colleague, Austin. We teach the same students, in the same high school, live 47 seconds from the building, and have united goals. It's awesome. He challenges me to step up to our Epic Adventure with confidence, even when I don't feel confident.

With that, I often feel I'm an unlikely human to change the world. I wasn't popular in school. Didn't stand out in a crowd. A follower in most activities. I was successful, of course, because I cared about doing a "good job," but I didn't have the gumption to extend myself too far. I took a few leadership roles the older I got, in a high school Bible study, campus sorority, and various ministries. I didn't think many of my positions mattered too much. I got married to a guy who I thought was way cooler and smarter than I was and we settled in a rural community. I'm not the stuff of heroes. But as I look at these stories, neither were they. Privet Drive was hardly on the map. The Shire was a quiet village on the way to somewhere else. Sure, Greatness can be a title, or it can be a mindset. I'm finding that the more I push myself, the higher my expectations for my life and career, the larger my sphere of impact and the more responsibility I have to my fellow humans. The goal is overwhelming, the task seems too impossible. Of course it is! The characters of these stories, you, me--we don't grow unless we are stretched and challenged. Humanity--people, culture, the classroom--can't change without some pressure. And in the end, it is always worth it.

I painted on my classroom walls several reminders from my favorite stories. It's a challenge to myself, and especially to my students, that they are the writers of their own Epic Adventure Stories. One of them is about choosing. It's about deciding to pack your satchel and follow the Grey wizard on an adventure. It's about caring enough to do something that matters. Dumbledore looks over his half-moon glasses, encouragingly: "It is our choices, Harry, that show us who we truly are, far more than our abilities."

So let us choose to take a risk. Let us be the faithful sidekick to our students. Let us challenge them to overcome. And in the process, we will compose our own Epic Adventure.

About Amanda Houp

Amanda is a small town High School English teacher, trying to make a big difference. She work with juniors and seniors in Ash Grove, Missouri, teaching English 3 and Composition and Literature. While her curriculum is American Literature and College preparatory reading and writing, she really tries to teach the arts of empathy, curiosity, personal responsibility.

Back in My Day

I wish there was a way to know you are in the good old days, before you've actually left them.

- Andy Bernard, *The Office*

"The Atomic Ant" My Inspiration

Leticia Carino

The first day I met my physical education teacher in high school. Her name was Aurora and I must say that I did not like her at all. Aurora was very strict and told us all how the rules would be enforced. At the time, I felt the rules were way too exaggerated. One example was that if you got to class one minute late, you would be facing some consequences.

Aurora was small, but quite strong. She couldn't sit still and was always engaged in some physical activity. In those days every teacher would drive to the high school. Not Aurora, she rode her bike every day despite the weather and ignoring the hills that were in between her house and the high school.

We used to call her " La Hormiga Atomica" "The Atomic Ant" because she was always doing some sort of exercise: Playing tennis, running, biking, swimming, and to date… she still is.

It felt like she put the bar quite high regarding her students' performance expectations.

That being said, my initial kind of negative opinion about Aurora, having us running outside even in the snow and being quite strict with us, changed in a single day.

I am from Madrid, Spain and therefore I studied in a public high school in a city called Majadahonda, in the outskirts of Madrid, where I used to live. As part of the physical education curriculum, PE teachers organised a field trip for us and, on this particular one, we travelled to the mountains to spend the day skiing. Since skiing is quite an expensive sport, I never had the chance to try it before, so the very first time I actually went to ski I was 15 years old.

I am not sure if you can remember your first day skiing, but in my case, I felt quite hopeless at the beginning, having to choose all the equipment, carrying heavy skis and poles while trying to find the best way to the meeting area. I took a chairlift with some friends up the mountain to go down the slopes but once I had arrived up the mountain, I realised I had no idea of how to ski or just how to get down safely.

Fortunately, one of my friends had some basic knowledge and she tried to teach me, but I kept falling down and losing my skis every time. If you have ever been in that situation you can picture how frustrating it is to try to go down the hill making some sort of triangle with your skis, and, as soon as you want to turn, you lose your balance and one ski goes down the slope, and you end up having to walk to get it, being careful that no crazy person is running you over as you try to get to where your ski is. Then you need to get all the snow off your boots, so you can actually click the skis back on again and try for the tenth time in 40 minutes to go down the green slope, especially made for beginners.

So there I was, after several attempts to go down the beginners slope and having fallen down multiple times, quite exhausted, more mentally than physically, and feeling quite upset with myself for not being able to ski, but how could I? Nobody trained me. I had just joined some friends on this field trip who were definitely more experienced than I was.

Anyhow, while I was about feeling ready to give up, Aurora, my PE teacher all of a sudden showed up. She told me that she was looking for me because she knew that I was a beginner, and from that moment on she stayed with me and my group of friends the whole day.

She taught me how to ski. She would patiently go slightly ahead of me on the slopes and outline the route for me the follow with her skis. She did it in such a way that it certainly gave me confidence and strength. She made me believe in my skiing learning ability that I was actually enjoying the day from then on.

After that day, my view on Aurora had completely changed. I realized that the reason why she could be very strict with us, especially at the beginning of the year, was to be respected, not to be mean to us. She did all sorts of things for us learners. One example was that she gave free after-school dance lessons, self-taught, so she could actually teach us.

When I was in my last year of high school, I wasn't really sure of what career I wanted to pursue. Finally I decided that I wanted to study Physical Education. In Madrid, in order to study Physical Education in College, you have to have a good grade in your admittance exam, plus you have to pass several fitness and physical tests that require quite some practice. I only learned at a very late stage that most people train for a year to pass those physical tests. I practiced for two weeks, with Aurora. As soon as she found out that I was thinking of studying Physical Education she offered her help.

The above mentioned tests include: swimming, endurance, strength, flexibility, agility, and several more. You must pass all the tests with the minimum grade (or higher) or you are out. No second chances.

The day of my physical tests was July 18th. It was really hot out there in Madrid. I was in quite good shape after two weeks of training my body non-stop.

I started very well, passing all the initial tests. There were two tests that I was feeling less confident about: Agility and Endurance. I had managed to pass the agility test and all of the other disciplines and now only had to face the endurance. We had to run one km in less than five minutes, and it was almost 6pm. It was really hot, but I didn't care. I knew I could do it. And I did!

Thanks to Aurora and her inspiration, I studied Physical Education, became a PE teacher and started to share the passion that she had shared with me with my students.

I have to say that like Aurora, I am firm in my classes, but at the same time care very much about my learners and their personal development. I am an advocate for health, physical activity and wellbeing not only with my students, but also with my colleagues and of course with my family, friends and the community.

I always have loved nature and the outdoors and that ski experience, really helped to guide me to who I am now.

I have become an international educator and I live in China now. Every summer I go back to Spain to spend time with my family and friends. Aurora and I became friends a long time ago. We get together to run in the forest close to where my parents live. Every summer we meet at the very same forest and run together as we catch up. She is always full of energy and we love to catch up and share with each other our life adventures.

Gracias Aurora, La Hormiga Atomica: You are my inspiration!

About Leticia Carino

Leticia studied Physical Education in Spain and taught it in Madrid for five years. In 2007 she and her husband moved to the US where she started her journey as an international educator. Since then, life has taken her to The Netherlands, and China where she lives now. In 2013 they adopted a baby from Ethiopia who fills their days with love. In July they are moving to Cambodia where she will be teaching PYP PE. Travelling and learning from other cultures is a passion of hers. She is an advocate for health and loves running, being outdoors, and getting lost in a good book.

An Idyllic Education - Nothing but Good Memories

Michelle Joyce

I grew up in a small farming community in Australia. No, it was NOT the Outback. Yes, I have seen a koala and a kangaroo. No, I do not say "Crikey!" or eat "shrimp on the barbie".

My nearest neighbors were about two miles away, but I had a lot of brothers and sisters so I was never lonely. Our family farm was just over 1000 acres, which was small by comparison to many of the others in the community, but large enough to be able to run wild, and play, and imagine, and explore. The town itself consisted of a general store that also housed the local post office and a single petrol bowser (gas pump). The people who ran the general store also were in charge of the train station (that only operated during harvest season for freight, never for passengers). They also drove the small school bus that travelled from farm to farm to deliver us to the local elementary school.

There were days when we were running late, or distracted by "Sesame Street" on the TV, when the bus driver had to honk on the horn to get us out of the house and onto the bus.

The school was a beautiful, century-old, bluestone building with walls thick enough to keep us cooler as the summer approached, but never felt warm enough, ever, during the winter months. It was a single room school house with one teacher for grades prep through six. (K-6) In the mornings I remember there was another adult present to help work with the "little kids" (K-2) but I was never sure of her status either as a part-time teacher or teacher's aide. The amount of organization and differentiation required by the teacher to keep everybody busy was not optional, it was a mandatory skill. As a consequence, we, the students, learned to be self-sufficient.

There were approximately 20 - 30 students in the school, and I was related to half of them. The community population was very stable for the most part and families had lived in the district for multiple generations. Everyone knew everyone and it wasn't an option to not get along. You were going to be with those people at least until the end of elementary school, and even though literally there was plenty of space, figuratively, there was nowhere to hide.

Once you graduated "from the carpet" (K – 2) to the main part of the classroom (3 – 6) much of the learning was coordinated independent study. There were workbooks for mathematics with lessons and practice to work at your own pace. I rarely remember getting assistance with math as I was always working far ahead of where any curriculum pacing guide would have placed me. The challenge was to see how far you could get ahead (even into the next year's work) before the teacher caught you and assigned other activities.

English had the SRA series of "reading laboratories" and a small workstation that had headsets so that those students at the same level, regardless of grade, could listen to the story without interrupting, or being interrupted by, the rest of the school. I remember tracing letters in the early grades with a thick blue pencil. Once you could trace the lines of the alphabet you graduated to slightly narrower lines. Letter formation was not my strong suit, patience in repetitive tasks is still not my strong suit. The next level of writing allowed you to move up to grey lead pencils (#2 pencils) and narrower lines once again. Once you reached whatever arbitrary level of skill in handwriting the teacher had determined, you were promoted to ink. That was a big day – and certainly one worth rushing off the bus when you got home to announce to your parents.

For social studies and science, all I really remember doing was reading books and completing projects.

The best part of the week were the media broadcasts. Once a week we listened to "Singing and Listening" on the radio and the whole school joined in the singalong. The little kids also got to listen to "Let's Join In" – a radio program targeted towards pre-reading skills, but still got them singing. On Fridays we were allowed to watch TV for a half hour for a special program called "Behind the News" (BTN). This news and current affairs program is still produced in Australia and has been running for almost fifty years. Looking at the BTN website now it is easy to see how much things have changed in education with the amount and variety of resources available online.

Of course all kids seem to love the PE the best. I remember having what seemed like endless recess in morning and again in the afternoon. Lunch required the first 10 minutes to be seated in the "shelter shed" and eat, and then again apparently unlimited time to run around and play. I am sure it wasn't unlimited, but it definitely felt ample to us as kids, and probably the only time that our solitary teacher ever had a few moments peace.

The skills I feel I learned from this unusual elementary school experience were:
- the independence it took to manage your own learning progress;
- the opportunity to be curious and pursue projects that were of interest to you;

- the responsibility one week per month to write your own timetable and schedule your lessons in your own personalized planner. Talk about organized chaos when every child was doing something different!

These organizational skills set me in good stead for planning my own studying in high school and college. The freedom gave me my passion for lifelong learning, and the responsibility for managing myself at an early age helped me become the strong, independent woman I have been my whole life.

It was quite a shock to graduate to high school (7 – 12) and attend a school that had about 600 students – effectively two classes of 25 at each grade level – each room pretty much more than my whole school for the previous seven years. The transition to college was even more intimidating – the campus having about 36,000 people onsite over the course of a week.

Idealized as I have presented my experience, I have nothing but good memories of the education I was provided. I respect and admire those first teachers who moulded my learning. Perhaps I was lucky in the teachers I had because some of my younger siblings relay their experiences quite differently, but I would recommend the "Little House on the Prairie" school system to anyone. In fact, my upbringing is part of the reason I homeschooled my son for the first few years. I wanted him to have the opportunity to learn through play, follow his interests, be outside as much as possible, and advance at his own pace, not one dictated by a class full of students of differing abilities.

So, I hope that my positive educational experiences translate on to my son and all "my kids". If learning is fun then it's easier to want to learn. When you want to learn, then it's easier to find your passions and pursue them. Imagine a classroom (or a world) where all participants were intrinsically motivated to do their best … I can dream … and I can do my small part to make it come true.

About Michelle Joyce

Michelle Joyce grew up in rural Australia, travelled the world for two years, and has lived and taught in Australia, India, England and the USA. She worked in a variety of careers to finance her travels, but returned to her passion and has been an educator for over 20 years in private and public schools. Michelle is currently teaching Chemistry, Physics and Thinking Skills in Florida.

A Reader's Tale

Lena Marie Rockwood

For as long back as I can remember, reading has been a huge part of who I am. I grew up on the second floor of a two-family house and my maternal grandparents lived on the first floor. My uncle, who was ten years older than me, lived there also.

My grandmother took care of me and set the expectations for attending to homework as soon as we got home from school. My uncle and I would have a special treat that she made and then we went right to work. Because he was ten years older, his books were much larger and his assignments much longer. The rule was the house was absolutely quiet and no television could be turned on until we were both done with our work. This is where my love for jigsaw puzzles also developed. The two things that could be done quietly while waiting was reading and assembling a jigsaw puzzle.

As a got older, I would spend a great deal of time at the public library. I grew up on Judy Blume books and looked forward to each new title to arrive. When I turned fourteen, I was hired as a library 'page' at my local branch. This involved making repairs to books, shelving and keeping books in order, helping patrons find books and reading some new titles to give recommendations. My favorite part of the job was being able to be the first to check out books. During college, I worked in the children's room of the main library branch where I fell in love with young adult novels. It was such a great feeling to be able to recommend a book to a child and have them come back to tell me all about it. There were families that came on the days I worked so we could pick the 'just right' book for the children.

I was not an education major when I entered college. I was a business major whose parents felt that becoming an educator was a thankless career that would not pay the bills. They were paying for my tuition so I accepted their guidance – I think forced to accept their guidance would be a better way to describe it as they said if I did not stick with the accounting major they would not pay for school. Midway through my junior year I was miserable and knew this was not the career for me. Around the same time, I met my husband. I ended up dropping out of college, getting married, and having children.

When my kids entered nursery school, the director noticed my interactions with other children. She offered me a job and after a couple of months signed me up for a few introductory education classes. This fueled the fire and I never looked back. It took me a while to get there but I got my degree and then went on to my master's and then a doctorate!

Books played a major role on each leg of the journey to complete my studies. I remember my first multicultural class where we needed to develop lessons. I created a resource of multicultural literature to be used at the middle grade levels. When needing to create a multidisciplinary unit, I chose The Celebrated Jumping Frog of Calaveras County by Mark Twain as the main reading and developed a three-week unit around this story. My undergraduate research professor required a "dissertation worthy" topic before he would approve our work in conducting a literature review. I remember not being happy that he was so particular but I thank him every day because that led to my actual dissertation study topic. You probably already know this was focused on reading and books too!

As a middle school teacher, I often used picture books as part of my lessons. The Butter Battle Book by Dr. Seuss was one of my favorites to share with middle schoolers. The students were always amazed with *How Much Is a Million* and often had a new perspective on the concept of a million after reading this book in middle school and remembering it as a younger child. As an administrator, I have created several family reading initiatives. My favorite was A Million Minutes of Family Reading. Families were encouraged to read together for fifteen to twenty minutes a day and log the minutes on a card. We tallied up the minutes and created math lessons on the percentages and many other curriculum connections along the way. The most rewarding moments of this initiative were the conversations with the adults who were readers before they had children but could not find the time to read. They found time each day to read and developed a routine for reading that became a habit. That was amazing!

I have had the unique opportunity to work as an administrator in an elementary and middle school in the same district where I have worked with many of the families for almost ten years. I have seen the children grow up! The one consistent memory that is often discussed when meeting up with parents and former students is the Million Minutes initiative. Many students remember how for twenty or more minutes the house was silent while everyone took time to read. Brings me back to my own younger years when the house needed to remain quiet until homework was done.

My passion for reading is still strong! I talk about books to students and teachers and anyone who will listen. When students in high school come back to visit, they usually ask me about what I am reading and we engage in a conversation about our recent favorites. They still try to convince me I will like the vampire themes but I am not convinced! I read as I monitor detention after school and students often ask what I am reading. I usually share the book when I am finished. I can't wait for new books to be released! I am on several email lists to receive 'book news' and probably spend as much time reading about books as I do reading actual books.

This passion led to the creation of the #Read4Fun Chat. There were four of us in a weekend chat when the topic of a book recommendation came up. Two of us mentioned Girl on a Train by Paula Hawkins and the other suggested Orphan Train by Christina Baker Kline (this is the short version of the story) so then the four of us created the chat. The collaboration around reading with Connie Rockow, Jen Williams, and Sean Gaillard was exciting! We even presented at The International Literacy Association Conference in July of 2016. As time goes by life usually pulls us in different directions and the same is true for the four of us. At the present time, I am moderating the chat myself and reach out to friends at #ShelfieTalk, #SixtyBooks, and the newly created #BookCampPD in addition to the #Read4Fun-ners as I like to call them. We chat on the first and third Sunday of the month and the topics vary. We engage on Twitter, Voxer and have been known to start a book discussion on either or both when we find a book we all want to talk about.

I would like to think that I would have developed this love for reading even if the house did not need to be quiet in order to finish homework. I am thinking that grandma really did know best when she implemented this rule!

About Lena Marie Rockwood

Lena is a Middle School Assistant Principal in Massachusetts. She is passionately curious and forever a learner. As a classroom teacher, she taught eighth grade science, middle school mathematics and study skills. She has coordinated science fairs at the school, district and regional levels. She loves to read, assemble jigsaw puzzles, crochet and sometimes knit. She believe in the power of positive mindset.

A Dime a Dozen

Anthony Virgilio

I am a high school graduate of the class of 2000. As I reminisce on my senior year, I recall the daunting tasks associated with the college application process. Meetings with my guidance counselor, writing application essays and above all, picking a major, were overwhelming for a seventeen year old adolescent whose mission in life was to "play with the band". I distinctly remember my initial college meeting. On that day, my guidance counselor presented me with a questionnaire that I was to use while deciding my major. I remember feeling anxious addressing serious questions about the "real" world. Questions such as:

What do I want to do with my life?

What are my strengths?

How much money would I like to make?

What are my career goals?

What are my passions?

Where do I see myself in twenty years?

When I began pondering these existential questions about who I was, and who I wanted to become, I was at a loss. At that age, I was more interested in my social life than my career path (as many high school students are). However, I was destined to attend college and earn a degree. I was a decent student who had maintained a respectable grade point average, scored well on the SAT exams and had the financial and emotional support of my parents. There was an expectation to attend college as well.

Of the questions listed above, the one that lead me to a career in education was "What are my passions?". I didn't know what I wanted to do with my life, but I knew what I loved.

I began playing guitar at the age of 13. I'll never forget the manner in which my father supported me when I expressed interest in the instrument. We went to a local music store and bought my first acoustic guitar the very same day I told him I wanted to learn. Typically I'd have to wait for an occasion in the form of a birthday or major holiday to receive an expensive gift. It was my lucky day.

As a tween I began taking private lessons and practicing for hours on end every day. Making music seemed to be "in my blood" and I felt I was destined to become a "Rock Star". During my freshman year of high school I formed what would become lifelong friendships with a few peers who agreed to form an original rock band. I continued to hone my musical skills by enrolling in every music elective I could and began jamming (rehearsing) with this band 4-5 days a week. We were determined to be successful.

By the time senior year came, my friends and I had established ourselves as the most popular local rock band in our mid-sized suburban town. We found ourselves playing in front of large audiences, selling compact discs (CDs) by the hundreds, getting invitations to house parties and running with the "in" crowd. It was an amazing time in my life.

Still, I had to answer some serious questions concerning my future. If my passion was music then it would seem logical to pursue a career in music performance, right? To reiterate, I wasn't entirely sure what I wanted to do with my life, but I knew my passion. Before submitting my college applications, I needed to gather opinions from my music teachers. I stopped by the music wing and began talking with a few of the music teachers in my school. What Mr. Joel said altered the path of my entire life...

Mr. Joel was a well-respected Jazz musician and a local teaching legend. He was a musician's musician, cool yet stern. He was the only teacher I've ever had that could make or break my day with just a look or a few words. Needless to say, he had a powerful aura and his blessing meant a lot to me. When I told him that I was going to become a music major he was excited for me, he asked, "what major are you considering?" When I told him my master plan of being a professional guitarist he looked at me in only a way he could and questioned my decision. He said, "Guitarists are a dime a dozen, you should become a teacher."

He began to list all the benefits that come along with the teaching profession - Steady work, inspiring the youth, building relationships, great union benefits, summers off etc... The longer I listened, the more sense this made.

After our conversation, I reluctantly applied to undergraduate school as an education major. One thing you have to understand about me is that I was, am, and always will be a dreamer. In 1999, I had plans to take the world by storm with my music. Education sounded like a good "fall back option" but it just didn't have the same allure. During undergrad school, I honestly considered music education to be my backup plan. The goal was to leverage collegiate course studies, better myself as a musician and run from the teaching profession as soon as my band got our big break. My band never became famous, but I did become a teacher.

Ten years down the line, education has brought more fulfillment to my life than I ever imagined it could and I'm grateful for the advice Mr. Joel gave me every day. I've established a love and passion for education that I never could have predicted; to the extent which I even have aspirations of becoming a school leader. I suppose we all have to let go of childhood dreams at some point.

I can't help but wonder if Mr. Joel knows the profound impact he had on my life. I respected the advice he gave me because I looked up to him. He was a role model. Teachers are role models. We as educators are among the most powerful influencers in the world and must be aware of the power of our words. Whether we realize it or not, students are always listening and one never knows when they will make a difference.

I thank you for reading and for doing what you do!

About Anthony Virgilio

Professionally, Anthony is a dedicated teacher with 10 years experience on Long Island, NY. Through the years he has taught students ranging from 6-12th grade in three different public schools. Although his content area is music, Anthony recently earned a master's degree in educational leadership and aspires to someday become an administrator.

In his personal life, Anthony is a proud husband and devoted dad. During his free time he enjoys reading, staying fit, playing guitar and spending time with friends.

Anthony is always looking to expand his professional learning network and values connecting with like-minded individuals. Connect with him on Twitter by searching for @AFVirgilio.

Best Day Ever

We didn't realize we were making memories, we just knew we were having fun.

\- Winnie the Pooh

"I just whispered to myself, This Is the Best Day Ever!"

Sophia Garcia-Smith

Just like every teacher in the world, there are days we feel overwhelmed. The pressures and expectations of teaching, testing, parenting and caring can make us question our sanity. It usually requires us to take a step back and have a moment that puts it all into perspective. I love my job, I love my students and I love what my teaching can do for them. This story is one of those moments.

Every day as a second grade teacher I am looking for ways to make learning fun and engaging. I remember being on Twitter when I saw a link to Caine's Arcade YouTube video. The tweet was using the hashtag #cardboardchallenge, this was enough to spark my interest. After watching the amazing video and following up with the story on the website, I was inspired. I knew that I needed to bring this inspiration and learning into my classroom. Like a lightning bolt I began to see connections of a cardboard arcade to our second grade balance and motion science unit.

A project based learning unit was born. The hardest and simplest part was that I had to change my way of teaching and thinking. This project was not about me and what I was teaching but about what the students were learning by creating. It took the students two weeks to create the most amazing arcade games using only cardboard, paper, tape and glue. The questioning, curiosity and scientific ideas that were generated made amazing concrete connections with my students.

We spent another week perfecting our writing and presentations that explained the science behind our games. They surprised themselves with the quality of their writing and scientific explanations were spot on. It was a proud moment for me to see how hard they were working to prove their science was connected to the games. We decided to take it a step further and record our presentations, turn them into QR codes and display them with the games. We shared our presentations on our blog and the response was mind blowing. We had students commenting on our work and our presentations from all over the country. We even received a tweet from Caine's Arcade, telling us what a great job we did. That was exactly what we needed to give us the confidence for the big day.

Finally the day arrived. The 2nd grade students invited the 1st grade and 3rd grade classrooms to come learn and play with the arcade games they had created. It was quite a sight to see and hear my students. They really got it! I heard amazing things like "This is not just a race track, do you know that it takes force and gravity to make this game work?" and "When you use forward motion it makes the ball go forward and gravity brings the ball down through the basket." As the morning went on and the compliments continued, I could see the pride in their eyes. A student was coming down the stairs after a bathroom break with a huge smile on his face, I asked him if he was having fun and he said "I just whispered to myself, this is the best day of my life". I swear if no one else had been around I would have broken down in tears of happiness. I decided then and there that no matter what, teaching and learning WILL continue to be FUN! I want to continue to hear that today is someone's best day ever.

About Sophia Garcia-Smith

Sophia Garcia-Smith is a Second grade teacher and also the mother to 3 beautiful teenage daughters. She teaches at Orchard Place School in Des Plaines IL. It is a Title 1 school that serves parts of Rosemont IL and Des Plaines IL. She loves integrating technology in her classroom and is always looking for new ways to make learning fun.

Worth it

Deborah Rodriguez

I've been addicted to archery since the first time I shot a bow, when I was eleven years old. My dad was my little brother's Cub Scout Den Leader and had allowed me and my sister to join the Den at an archery outing. I remember being fascinated by all the new things, but that the best part was yet to come. They began to teach the lesson and the Rangemaster realized that the bow they had given me was too small. I remember thinking, I'm a girl, but I get a bigger bow! The fact that I'm two years older than my brother being the reason hadn't occurred to me. I trotted up the path to the Range building and informed the person in charge that I needed a bigger bow, and I was hooked.

My dad ran ranges for my Girl Scout troop after that, and as I got older I could help. I became adept at recognizing errors and correcting them quickly and efficiently, always being sure to keep my voice measured and calm so as not to distract the other archers. I learned from my dad how to give 'the look' that lets new archers know that their behavior is inappropriate for the range and which silences groups within seconds of its administration. And I learned that archery is an activity in which ANY participant may become successful, as long as they possess the patience and willingness to try.

I went out the second I turned 18 to get my Level 1 training, and at 21 years of age, I attained Level 2. Being able to run ranges was awesome, but being able to teach other adults how to run ranges safely? Even better! I ran trainings about once a year for my summer camp and then ran ranges for various weekend and summer programs just because I loved it. Sometimes it was volunteer and sometimes it was paid, but it was always a blast.

Over the years my methods improved. My safety speech became shorter and more concise, and my students improved more quickly under my tutelage, even if they only had one hour once with me and 19 other rambunctious campers. I ran more trainings through other groups: a Girl Scout service unit here, a Boy Scout council there. I learned a lot about the value of my knowledge and my willingness to share it. I became a teacher, and the archery trainings dwindled a bit as my schedule was busy enough without adding extra school year volunteering. I switched schools and learned that the new school had an archery unit in the PE class and the wheels began to turn again. If they have an archery range, I thought, then I can teach an archery club here. I raised the idea to a couple of teachers, and students soon found out about the idea and searched me out. Shortly thereafter I had a small dedicated group of interested students, all raring to go.

The big hang up was the equipment. It wasn't that the equipment they had was unsafe, per se, but 15 years is a long time to use the same exact equipment! I met with the PE teacher, and upon seeing the school's equipment, my feeble dream of an archery club was dashed. I hadn't taught on that kind of equipment in 13 years, and I was NOT going back to those days. The newer styles of equipment are safer, and let's just be honest, BETTER. I just wasn't willing to risk it. The Archery Club idea was dead before it could even start.

And then it wasn't. I had the thought: If only I had my own equipment, I would be able to teach archery whenever I want to. I could run trainings, weekend camp activities, and the club idea could continue. I let the thought percolate. I mean, why couldn't

I have my own set of archery equipment? I asked myself. It's expensive, I told myself. But it's doable, I answered. I debated for a couple of weeks, and reached out to my camp friends. I asked them if people would support me if I decided to open a business. How hard could it possibly be? The response was overwhelmingly positive. Of course they would support!

So I started a GoFundMe. I picked up extra hours at work. I helped a neighbor organize and pack for a move. I offered incentives of teaching archery once the business would start up and for other crafty things that a 19 year veteran of the Girl Scouts can do. For three months I struggled and wheedled and tried. And I made it.

I ordered the bows and the arrows and the arm guards, and I printed applications to join the club for my interested students. I required them to have no F's and to get teacher recommendations to join the club and to write a paragraph about why they wanted to join the club. I made sure I had safety lines and all necessary precautionary gear and a first aid kit, and I special-ordered a safety poster that I designed myself.

The first day of the club meeting was a Friday, about a month before the end of the school year. What a time to start a club! I think I was more excited even than the students, but when they all filed in, I was ecstatic. I showed them how to put together the bows, which is something I've never entrusted to students before that moment. I've only ever had adults learn how to assemble bows, but I needed to prepare them to help, since we'd be waiting forever if we waited for me to put everything together by myself.

The larger bows are easier to put together and the stronger students use them, so we had to wait for the medium bows to be assembled. I taught them which gear they needed and we gathered up everything to go out to the range. We set the range up with safety lines and the poster and the targets and after almost half of our appointed time was already gone, we finally were ready.

For the safety speech, I've given it a million times, but these kids were MINE. More than any group I had ever taught before in the 11 years since my Level 1 certification training, I felt like these kids NEEDED archery. I looked at the eager faces of students who had never tried archery before (minus the one Boy Scout) and felt it in my bones that they wanted to succeed. It was the best safety presentation I had ever given.

They lined up, bows in hand, and I walked them through the shooting process. Each of them had the best smile as they shot for the first time ever, and it was perfect. They retrieved their arrows without a single issue, and as I blew the whistle to allow them to shoot the second time, I realized.

I realized that I had started a business in order to bring a new opportunity to my students. I laughed, accidentally startling the nearby newly taught archers, and then I looked around. The wind was blowing, but the arrows were flying true. The students were hitting the targets with that satisfying THWACK that I loved, and I was teaching ARCHERY at my school where I was hired to teach Spanish.

And I started to get tears in my eyes. If there was ever any doubt in my life about whether or not I was in the right profession, it was dashed from my mind in that moment. I started a business to volunteer to teach my students, my kids, my hobby.

About Deborah Rodriguez

Deborah Rodriguez is a fourth year Spanish teacher in West Sacramento at River City High School. In her spare time, she plays chess, teaches archery, and constantly looks for other new hobbies to fill her 'copious spare time'. Roller derby, running and playing with her puppy Reina are at the top of her current hobby list, but she'll also always be a Girl Scout volunteer as well.

The Grouchies

Ann Kozma

I seriously just won the day… at least it feels like that.

Today started like most other days. A 7:15 am stop at Starbucks for an iced coffee classic with cream…then, on to a school site for a demo lesson. You see, I am not a regular classroom teacher. I am what is called a TOSA - a Teacher on Special Assignment. I work in the Fullerton School District in Fullerton, California and support teachers and students with the innovative and instructional use of technology. I absolutely love my job. People ask all the time, "Do you miss the classroom?" The truth is, I do. I miss making deep connections with a group of students over the course of a school year. But, truth be told, I still get to make connections with students, in all the classrooms that I visit. Days like today reinforce the fact that I don't have to be in my own classroom to make an impact with students.

Two days ago, I was working with a group of teachers when a side conversation about positive behavior reinforcements came up. I shared a favorite lesson I used to do in my classroom that reinforces positive behaviors and one of the teachers said, "Can you do that in my classroom…like tomorrow?" We made an immediate plan for me to return in two days to teach this lesson while introducing a new tech tool to her Kindergarten students.

Which brings us back to today.

I walked into Mrs. V's room and was greeted by her smile. She is caring, creative and has the sweetest way with her young scholars. Student learning is evident when you look around her classroom. I've spent a few days working with her students this year, so I felt like I already had a connection to her students. When her students walked in, I was greeted with gasps of joy and excitement. One student said, "Miss Kozma is here!" Another asked, "Are we doing iPads with you?"

I told them that we would be reading a book and responding to it while learning how to use an app called Doodle Buddy. I explained to students that the book I was going to read to them, The Grouchies by Debbie Wagenbach, used to be an app on my iPad but that just last night when I went to open the app it wasn't working. They looked at me, a bit puzzled. So, with some funny movements, I explained that every time I launched the app it would open, then immediately shut down...open, then shut down. We giggled a little bit and I'm sure they were probably wondering how in the world were we going to be able to read The Grouchies if we didn't have the actual book and the app wouldn't even work. I explained to them that I did have a few pictures of pages from the book and we would read from those, but that we wouldn't be able to read the whole book. They agreed that that was ok and so we began.

We started the lesson talking about the illustrations on the cover of The Grouchies. The illustrator, Steve Mack, created a beautiful book jacket to illustrate that the "Grouchies" are little, angry clouds that surround us and affect our mood. With some more funny movements and a challenge to show me their "grouchiest" faces and their happiest faces, we began to read. This book is a brilliant story of a little boy who, from the moment he wakes up, is influenced by the Grouchies and has a hard time controlling his emotions, his actions, and the way he interacts with his friends and family. Throughout our reading, we paused to reflect on the emotions our main character was feeling, how he was reacting and treating others, and whether or not those were good choices. By the midpoint of the book, we knew that this little boy was having a really hard day, just like another little boy who once had a terrible, horrible, no good very bad day.

At this point in the lesson, I paused. Really, I didn't have any more pictures of pages from the book. So, we used chart paper and brainstormed ideas for how this little boy could chase the Grouchies away. Students responded with great ideas like singing, dancing, drawing a picture, using kind words, being nice to others, and sharing. One little girl said that she should use the "power of friendship." A little boy reminded us of the Golden Rule. We moved into a short conversation about our own emotions and feelings and how we feel when the Grouchies take control. We all agreed that it is more fun to be happy and smile than to frown and fuss and let the Grouchies win. I did have one more page from the book to share with the students. It was the last picture and it shows the little boy, waking up the next morning, surrounded by sunny smiles instead of being surrounded by gloomy Grouchies. The same girl who had talked about the "power of friendship" called out that the sunny smiles looked like emojis. We all laughed and agreed.

Now, as a TOSA, my job is to help teachers see how to meaningfully integrate technology into their classrooms. So, I decided to use the Doodle Buddy app and lead students in a digital art lesson and guide them through the process of drawing their very own Grouchie. Since these students are new to using iPads in their classroom, I know that systematically teaching the workflow of an app is a great way to help them learn how to effectively use it. Doodle Buddy has a few powerful and versatile tools embedded within the app. I first taught the students how to change the background paper and then to use the stamp tool. They were excited to have a few minutes to play with the stamp tool. During those moments, Mrs. V and I discussed the potential ways she could use Doodle Buddy in her classroom. I love to embed coaching into demo lessons and blending the learning for both teachers and students. These few minutes of exploration and play allowed for students to push buttons, independently figure out how to use tools within the app, and see possibilities for their own creation and own their learning. These few minutes also provided me with the chance to answer questions the teacher had, share my ideas for best practices, tips and tricks and observe with her as her students figured out how to use the app and collaborate to solve problems. I moved the lesson along and introduced the drawing tool to the students, helped them learn how to change the color and change the drawing tool from brush to chalk to glitter. I modeled how to draw a Grouchie and then let them work independently as I moved around the room to provide help when needed.

"Look!"

"I did it!"

"I made a Grouchie!"

We celebrated the success these students were experiencing by creating an impromptu art gallery. I learned about the idea for an impromptu gallery from Cathy Hunt in her closing Keynote at CUE17. I had yet to make an impromptu gallery with students and I knew this would be the perfect opportunity. We arranged the iPads on the floor, placing them into a 5x5 grid, and we stood around them and admired the creative work. This was a simple and spectacular way to celebrate success. Students loved seeing their work "showcased" and loved seeing what their peers had made.

It was in these moments that I looked at Mrs. V and we just smiled. Something special had happened during this lesson. Students were allowed to explore their feelings and emotions as they responded to literature. Students were empowered as they learned how to use a new app on their iPad devices. Students took ownership of their learning and used technology to create their own personalized response to the story. Student success was celebrated and honored in an impromptu gallery that allowed each child to feel valued. So many little things came together and every student was engaged and focused on their work. Beyond all that, a few other things were happening.

"I was never interested in having an iPad one to one class until today. This has been one of the best, if not the best day, possibly of my entire teaching career." Mrs. V said these words to me and they filled my heart and reminded me that the hard decision I had made, to leave the classroom and become a TOSA, was the right thing for me to do. I have the great privilege of supporting teachers as they learn how meaningful technology integration can impact and influence both teaching and learning. Lessons like this remind me of those aha moments I got to experience with my students...now I experience them with teachers too.

The best part of today is that this is just the beginning. I get to continue to walk alongside this teacher and support her in exploring new ways to use technology and integrating practices into her classroom.

The smiles from today made me feel like I won the day...and fuel me to keep going.

About Ann Kozma

Ann Kozma is a Teacher on Special Assignment in Fullerton, CA. After 10 years teaching in the classroom, Ann stepped into the TOSA role in order to help others with the innovative and instructional use of technology. She is an Apple Distinguished Educator, Leading Edge Certified Professional Learning Leader, CUE Rockstar Lead Learner and has earned the Google Level 2 certification. Ann is driven by the words explore, share, and contribute and believes that play is our brain's favorite way of learning. Catch an EDU Story or connect with Ann on social (@annkozma723) or read her occasional blog at techtravelteach.com.

A Decade's Worth of Love

Emily Langerholc

May 4th, 2017 may have possibly been my favorite day of my career so far. We held our Spring Concert that night. It seemed almost impossible to clear students off campus afterwards because my students were hugging and crying so much. I carried the bouquet of roses that a parent had presented me with as my students hugged me. Although it had been a stressful school year in an increasingly difficult field, that concert made me remember why I loved being a teacher. It wasn't so much the musical achievements of my students, although they performed very well, or even the love they showed me after the performance. I was moved by the love they have for each other.

As per tradition, during the concert I passed out a small eighth note pin to each of my eighth graders toward the end of the concert. Many of them hugged me as I gave them their pins, and even more of them started crying at that point and didn't stop for another half hour. It is wonderful to know that your students love you, but it is more gratifying to know they love each other. To be responsible for that kind of environment is the thing I'm proudest of, and that which keeps me going throughout the very long hours and strenuous workload.

It is easy to get caught up in the many demands of teaching, especially teaching in an active and visible medium such as music. It is also easy to get caught up in self doubt and become disconnected to your work.

I have always been plagued by self doubt. And these days, I have good reason to be tired often. If teaching both band &

chorus were not enough of a workload, I also have a two-year-old daughter and a mother with limited mobility disabilities. I feel frequently overwhelmed these days, and I question my professional effectiveness often.

On the night of May 4th though, I felt rooted in what I do for a living, much more so than usual. I remembered exactly why the work I put into our music program is worth the struggle. I came home to my husband and sleeping daughter, buzzing with renewed purpose.

Most full school concerts come and go, twice a year, sometimes producing magic, sometimes producing mayhem. I had not felt quite so rooted in my career, however, since the first school concert of my career.

December 18th, 2007 was the night of my first full school concert as a director. There was a lot of love to be had that night. It was my first concert not only as a brand new director but as a the new director at that school. My administration was thrilled with my approach to the program, and the parents seemed to love me, too. Even the high school director down the street had high praise for my concert and my kids. I received at least one bouquet of roses from parents.

But instead of taking them home to my family, I brought my roses back to my empty apartment. I sat and stared. I didn't have my family nearby. I didn't have my friends nearby. I didn't have a supportive partner asking me about how things went. I had just moved three hours south of home. I'd left everything behind for a relationship that had just ended in a sudden and emotionally devastating manner. That took place on December 14th, 2007. Once I left school on the 18th (and every night from then on), I was all alone.

But four days after the break-up, having just come home from that first concert (and a 14-hour day at school), I felt that first intense post-concert sense of purpose. I found myself sitting at my dining room table of my tiny apartment, getting up only to put the roses I'd received in a makeshift vase. The ex had known how much I had been stressing leading up to this concert, my first as a fully fledged band director, and still dropped the biggest bomb he could have, four days prior, regardless.

As I sat at that empty table that night with my roses, I didn't think about my fresh heartbreak. I thought about my job, I thought about my kids, and I thought about my co-workers. I thought about how grateful I was to be a band director, and how grateful I was to work with those particular students. And although everything else in my life at that moment felt like it was in freefall, the aftermath of that concert that night was enough to keep me rooted.

I could have fled home after the breakup. I could have come home to the people who loved me. I would have saved a lot of money and been well-taken care of. But I decided that night that I wasn't going to turn around and run home with my tail between my legs. I wasn't going to let myself be beaten down by a bad case of abandonment. My kids, my school, my program needed me. And I needed them just as much. So I stuck it out, although I felt stranded far away from all of the people I loved most. I was rooted in my work, in my teaching, in the world of my students.

A few years on, I found myself rewarded for hanging on. Although the stats always paint a picture of teachers leaving the field within their first five years, I continued to hang on. Along the way, I met my magnificent husband, had my mother move down south with us, earned my master's degree in a fantastic program, and my husband and I welcomed our daughter in 2015. For as much as I still miss my home, I know that these wonderful things would not have happened had I turned tail and gone home after the big breakup. I am forever grateful that I made that decision, ten years ago, to stay put and give everything I had to my students.

Ten years on, I still reflect gratefully on that decision. A decade is a marker of time for a reason; I have survived many professional obstacles and held on, just as I decided to that night in 2007. On May 4th, 2017, I had the clearest evidence ever that I was intended to be a teacher and that holding fast to my teaching career had brought other brilliant blessings into my life.

Throughout my career, I have not received the professional consideration or the awards that I had hoped for when I was younger. My bands have not gotten the ratings I've hoped for at assessments, and there are a lot of ways in which I feel I have been overlooked. Sometimes that gets me down. But after May 4th, after all of the love I've been privy to over the course of my teaching career, I start to remember why I teach. There can be so many types of love that we experience in our lives, and I am lucky enough to pursue the love I experience in my teaching career, to have the love in my family, and to bear witness to the love my students have for each other.

About Emily Langerholc

Emily Langerholc teaches middle school music in Palm Beach County, FL. She directs Band, Chorus, and oversees an after-school Rock Band club. She has degrees from the University of Central Florida and Florida State University. She believes in music for music's sake and in the possibilities of popular music in the classroom.

Go to the Principal's Office

If you want to build a ship, don't drum up the men to gather wood, divide the work, and give orders. Instead, teach them to yearn for the vast and endless sea.

—Antoine de Saint-Exupéry

Appreciation Matters

Amy Illingworth

Being an elementary principal is as close to being a rockstar as I'll ever be. Walking around campus and hearing students call out, "Miss I!" was so much fun!

When I was principal, our school had a Friday Flag event each and every Friday morning. The entire school community met on the back playground where we did the pledge of allegiance, made announcements, and where one class would lead us in a song for the week. These songs were often patriotic or fun kid-pop songs that we all knew the words to. This was one of the ways in which we built our community.

Each Friday I would make my way to the back of the school after finishing my morning supervision out front. [Don't be jealous of the glamorous life of a principal!]

On this particular Friday I was the last to arrive out back. All of our students were gathered with their teachers and many of their parents, in a large semi-circle. There was our usual flag and microphone set up ready and waiting for me to begin. Only, before I could reach the microphone, a teacher was holding it and beginning her own announcement.

I can't remember exactly what she said, but I remember that I began to cry almost immediately. She quickly explained that today was now known as "Miss I day," and that today they were all here to appreciate me. All of a sudden, each class held up a sign the students had made. I saw "We love you!" and "Miss I-nspirational!" and many other cute messages on banners around the playground.

After the announcement, a group of teachers came up to the front and sang a song. But this was not one of our usual Friday Flag songs. The staff had rewritten lyrics to "Walking on Sunshine" to be all about me. This was an inside joke that showed just how well my staff knew me. They knew that I had worked at Chuck E. Cheese as a teenager and that "Walking on Sunshine" was the song I was required to memorize a dance routine to as part of my job.

Hearing my hard-working teachers sing a song they had written to thank me for being leader was overwhelming.

When I returned to the office, still wiping away the tears of joy and gratitude, I was met by yet another surprise. My office staff were all wearing the same t-shirt, and the shirt had a picture of me on it! They had made their own appreciation shirts to wear just to make me laugh!

One of the best days I ever had was when my staff planned an appreciation day for me! But it wasn't because it was a day all about me. This day helped me see the impact I was making as a leader. Leaders know how important trust is when building relationships.

Three years earlier, I came to this school as a brand new principal, new to the district, new to the elementary level, and just plain NEW. I worked hard to get to know the staff and I struggled with how to let them get to know me. We, collectively, worked hard to support our students, many of whom came from rough situations outside of school.

As we got to know each other on behalf of the challenging work we shared, I learned how valuable appreciation can be. Leaving a simple hand-written note to thank a staff member for doing something didn't take much of my time, but it brought me closer to individuals. Making sure that each of my weekly bulletins and Friday Flag announcements included some note of appreciation for a job well done by a student, a parent, or a staff member, became invaluable.

Receiving a thank you from a staff member or a hand-drawn card from a student also meant a lot. Being an elementary principal is a very isolating job. During most of my time as a principal I did not have any assistant principals, counselors, or other administrative support working alongside me. I relied heavily on my amazing secretary, my dedicated head custodian, my literacy coach, and my lead teachers for support with academic and operational tasks.

I tried to acknowledge hard work and dedication as much as possible, but it is never enough. Educators today work harder than any other profession, in my opinion. We serve as the teachers, counselors, nurses, therapists, parents, friends, and coaches for hundreds of students every year. We work long beyond "contract hours" and our work follows us everywhere- sometimes in the form of stacks of papers to be graded and other times as a sleepless night spent worry about a homeless student and his or her family in crisis.

What I learned from "Miss I" day was that appreciation matters. No matter the role you play, please take time to share your appreciation with your colleagues, your mentors, your friends in the trenches with you, doing this work that is a calling for us all. Appreciate big and small things. Appreciate a kind gesture, a smile in a busy hallway, a functioning PLC, an empathetic leader, a supportive colleague, and anything else that helps you be the best you can be for our students every day.

I appreciate each and every educator I've worked with and learned from. I appreciate each educator who is reading this collection of stories. Thank you, from the bottom of my heart.

About Dr. Amy Illingworth

Amy is currently the Director of Professional Growth in the Sweetwater Union High School District in south San Diego county. She has served as a district leader, site principal, assistant principal, literacy coach, and teacher in public education for 20 years. She blogs at:

https://reflectionsonleadershipandlearning.wordpress.com/ and can be found on Twitter @AmyLIllingworth.

Respect and Grace

Antonio Romayor Jr.

The year of 2008. The economy in California, and throughout the world, was in shambles. Stress levels were extremely high. Districts struggled to keep their budgets balanced. Even after reducing programs, cutting discretionary spending and reducing costs, districts were forced to lay off large numbers of employees. My district was no different. During a District Management Meeting, leadership shed tears as they described the significant cuts the district would have to enact to stay solvent. A co-worker would later describe the cuts, as "the removal of appendages." As "cutting away the hands and feet of the culture" that made up our district. As vivid as that sounds, it was exactly how we felt.

In the weeks that followed, leadership met with department heads to discuss the budget cuts. Up to this point, the Technology discretionary budget had been drastically reduced, but staffing levels remained the same. During the turmoil, a Technology employee decided to take another job, which accomplished the budget reductions needed at the time. However, that would quickly change.

It was a Saturday, about 10 am. I received an email from the Superintendent while enjoying breakfast with my family. The email was brief, but the impact would not be. The budget situation had worsened. "Worsened?", I remember thinking. "How can it get worse?" "Please review the attached file," the email read. I reviewed the file. I remember thinking, "Where am I going to cut an additional $70,000? I don't have that much discretionary funds." That's when it hit me. Swiftly and suddenly, like an unexpected punch to the gut. I would have to lay off an employee.

I felt sick to my stomach. The department was already severely understaffed. The position left vacant by the previous Information Technology Specialist had not been filled, and wouldn't be. At the time, in addition to myself, the department consisted of only two other employees. "How can I decide which employee to layoff?," I recall saying to myself. At this point in time, all classified and management employees were being furloughed several days a year, everyone's medical benefit costs were skyrocketing, and step-raises had been frozen. It was one of the hardest decisions I would have to make as a young administrator. Yet, I was determined to find a way to avoid laying anyone off. I met with leadership to discuss funding options. Together, we came up with a good solution. However, the decision would require Board action. The stakes were high, and emotions ran even higher.

The night of the Board meeting couldn't come soon enough. I sat in the back row of the Board Room, along with the employee that was being considered for layoff. While we were confident our solution could work, we understood what was at risk. The Board would have to take exception with this single employee. It felt like an insurmountable request considering the number of other employees possibly losing their job. We waited, one agenda item at a time, until it was time for the action item pertaining to my co-worker. I explained the solution and the justification for my request. The Board began to deliberate. The Board was having a difficult time justifying the exception. Over 30 employees, including teachers, were being laid off. It came time for the vote. One by one, the Board members decided the fate of my co-worker. "Yay," the first Board member said. "Nay. Nay," the following two Board members said. I remember the strain on my soul, and the look on my co-workers face as our confidence dissipated. The stress was palpable that night. It filled the room, and everyone in attendance felt it. The final two Board members voted. "Yay. Yay,.." they said. The final vote tally was 3-2, in favor for not laying off my co-worker. With confusion and despair on his face, my co-worker turned to me and asked, "So? What does that mean?" I exhaled in exhaustion and said, "You're good."

The following morning I met with leadership. We needed to discuss the solution in more detail. I was frustrated, and it showed. My words were uncharacteristically judgemental, and short. I couldn't believe what had transpired the night before. Rather than focusing on the positive, I focused on the negative. The stress of the entire ordeal was cascading out of my mouth, and into the ears of the the Associate Superintendent. He could sense my concern, and rather than correct my bad behavior, he offered insight. "Respect and grace," he said. "No matter what happens, all we can do is act with respect and grace - in everything we do."

I paused...as we tend to do when we suddenly realize we're making a mistake. "You're right," I expressed with embarrassment and lament. I learned a valuable lesson that day. A lesson that changed my approach to administration forever. No matter the situation, the obstacle or difficulty, leaders must continue to lead. Not just with action, but also with intent. An intention motivated by respect for the culture and systems which govern our organizations. Always acting gracefully with others, no matter the circumstances. A leader is defined by his or her attitude towards adversity, not by the adversity itself.

Leadership qualities are forged. A person in a position of leadership must exercise their character in trials and tribulation. How else can their qualities and virtues develop and strengthen? However, not everyone is successful in developing leadership qualities and virtues. At times, the adversity can drive people to dig their heels deeper or cling on to notions they believe to be right and just. It's my opinion that the only way to avoid a stunt in leadership growth is by creating and nurturing mentorship relationships with leaders that have passed successfully through trials, and emerged stronger and more energized. The vitality of a leader that leads with respect and grace is directly connected to his or her ability to maintain an open mind to change, criticism and adversity, while maintaining a humble sense of purpose, healthy self-esteem and a sincere concern for the people they lead.

In the years that followed, the economy in California, and around the world, began to improve. Employees previously laid off were coming back to work. Districts began to hire more staff, and new programs were implemented. Eventually, employees would receive raises - some even bonuses, to help make up for furloughs and frozen salaries. The Great Recession affected everyone differently. Many lost their homes, countless others were left unemployed and entire industries were lost. Amidst the pain, the suffering and the financial turmoil, educators continued to instruct students. Educational leaders continued to plan and prepare teachers. Families continued to prioritize their child's education.

Since the recession, economists, industry experts and even movie producers have attempted to explain what exactly led up to the recession and how it can be avoided in the future. Countless personal lessons about the recession have been shared and heard. As for myself, I too learned a valuable lesson - attitude makes a significant difference. By embracing a different attitude, I forged lasting and valuable partnerships. Partnerships that continue to pay high-dividends. Dividends that directly impact the students of El Centro Elementary School District, and it's employees.

About Antonio Romayor Jr.

The Chief Technology Officer for El Centro Elementary School District, a TK-8th grade district located in Imperial County. Antonio's responsibilities include creating and providing training on technology integration strategies for teachers and administrators to support the district's overall mission of "ensuring each student reaches exceptional academic achievement every day.

Outside the Box

If you don't love something, you're not going to go the extra mile, work the extra weekend, challenge the status quo as much.

- Steve Jobs

The Practice and Magic of Gratitude

Corrie Myers

I am so grateful for Senior Ditch Day. I know it's probably not professional of me to say that, but it's the truth. Let's me explain.

In just a few weeks, our school's first graduating class will walk across the stage and receive their diplomas. I've been with these students since they started as tiny little freshmen, so every time I've taught this particular class of students (which is three out of the four possible times), I've wanted the experience to be better than before. With an enthusiastic, passionate partner teacher by my side, we set out to plan senior curriculum that mattered to now and their future in every way possible.

So when the seniors decided to take senior ditch day earlier than the typical senior takes (you know, on a day when they're supposed to be in school), Sarah and I decided to convert this day into a quasi-planning day. We corralled our collective eight students into one classroom, pushed our two desks and minds together and got to planning our first final exam.

Up to that point we had the units planned out. We share our curriculum on a shared Google Drive, and we have one Google doc planning template we use to carve out every day of the school year. But despite our best intentions, we were left with about four days without instruction or assessment, including the final for that trimester.

This was the problem we were trying to solve on that first day of November when our seniors were recovering from a night of pretending they were young enough to still parade around neighborhoods chomping on medium-sized Snickers and little boxes of Nerds. How do we make four days of instruction and assessment meaningful, challenging, and relevant to our seniors?

So we got to thinking. What were the life skills, concepts, or themes that we had felt impacted us as adults? If we're trying to prepare our seniors to be ready for what lies ahead post high school diploma, what does that practically look like? How can we help them become healthy individuals?

Somewhere in this conversation, we decided on the concept of gratitude. We had watched Dr. Brené Brown's popular TED Talk on vulnerability and how gratitude is a practice of living wholeheartedly. Which is to say, we knew that this concept was deeper than we typically give it as a society. We thought we'd have them write letters of gratitude, but that felt normal. Certainly that is something they had done in the past. And we wanted to push them in new ways because we knew that in order for this experience to be impactful it needed to be challenging and a bit unfamiliar.

After some googling and drafting of a lesson plan on a Google doc, we figured out our plan. Modeled after a Soul Pancake video, we decided this would be the flow of our "make it count three day unit."

Day 1: Learn about the power of gratitude. Use research-based studies and practice gratitude by writing on sticky notes, creating a collective mural of thank you notes.

Day 2: Write a letter of gratitude to three people: a family member, a friend, and a teacher/staff member from any point in their high school career. Bring in materials and create a DIY token of gratitude for ONE of those three people.

Day 3: Surprise! Take those letters and instead of sending them in the mail or forgetting them, pull out your phone and call the person. On camera.

To be candid, we really didn't know how this would go. Even up until that last second before we told high school students in 2017 that they were going to face their worst fear and pick up the phone and call someone, we weren't sure.

I remember stepping out into the pod that joins our two classrooms and flagging Sarah down before we started. We stood outside our classrooms and wondered if we could really do this. Actually, we wondered if our seniors would show up to this. We were asking them to be vulnerable, and to have that vulnerability recorded. We nodded our heads in agreement that it was too late to go back, so we left the pod with the cameras ready for action and walked back into our respective classrooms to reveal the surprise.

We asked the students to take out their letters of gratitude. We asked generally what they thought we were going to do with them. They all assumed we were going to mail them to the recipients. So we showed them the video that inspired the lesson, the video where four people write letters of gratitude and then, surprise, are asked to call the people on the phone. It's an emotional video, one that leaves you feeling tender and hopeful.

Then we said, take out your letters. And your phones. You're going to call the three people you wrote to. On camera.

The combination of their generation that avoids phone calls like the plague and the vulnerability of the task itself sucked the confidence out of the room. They weren't afraid, necessarily, but unnerved for sure. I told them they could go whenever they were ready, that I would be waiting in the pod for the next person to call, but that everyone need to call on camera that class period. That was their final exam. While they waited for their phone call, they worked on their DIY tokens of gratitude.

One of my seniors boys volunteered to go first. He called his mom. Within this first call, I knew that this was different than anything I had experienced, both as a teacher and as a person. Watching the progression of their nervousness, their love, their gratitude, insecurity, and immense joy cannot be captured in words alone. I've tried on multiple occasions to trace the steps of that experience but words fail me every time.

This first student, as with every student after him, stepped up to the occasion. In the quietness of the room, with me, the camera, and their phone, it was up to them to make this experience matter. And they did. Many students cried, as did their recipients. Every single student left with a deep sense of gratitude. Each one changed the person on the other end for the better. While we recorded calls on camera, the rest of the students turned my classroom into Santa's Workshop, building and gluing the sweetest tokens of gratitude. And if they weren't working on that, they were pacing the walkway making more phone calls, heart beckoning them to keep going, keep sharing gratitude.

While each phone call was an individual experience, it became a unifying bond between peers. Being vulnerable and open caused them to be kinder, more empathetic-- with others and themselves.

This #GratitudeWorkshop, as we called it, had a domino effect. The magic of this final exam was that it permeated every person involved. It created a connected space for every staff and student on campus willing to say yes.

It was a risk. We couldn't test this experiment out, we just had to go for it. In order for The Gratitude Workshop to be successful, we had to trust that our students understood the value in what we were asking them to do. We had to trust that they would take this risk right alongside us.

I learned so many valuable lessons through this experience, and high on the list is the personal value I found in practicing gratitude.

But as a teacher, this lesson taught me to view even the most narrow and rigid of structures-- final exams-- and be willing to listen, be willing to turn convention on its head to discover something beyond my deepest imagination.

About Corrie Myers

Corrie Myers is a high school English teacher in Carlsbad, CA. She's been teaching for eleven years but feels more excited about the profession than when she started at age 22.

A Year In Review

Casey Korder

My 11th year educating learners in the Clark County School District in Las Vegas, Nevada is quickly coming to an end. I'm fearful of what the future holds.

At the end of last year my wife and I...

Yes, we are both educators working at the same school and in the same grade level. We had just completed two incredible years of looping, following our students for two years, with our 2nd and 3rd grade learners. We capped that off with our marriage in March and the birth of our first child in May of 2016.

...were called into the principal's office. Not only was the principal there, so was the assistant principal. We were both wondering:

"Uh oh."

"What is this all about?"

"Did we do something wrong?"

They both asked us what grade level we wanted to teach the following year. We expressed we wanted to keep looping with our students; However, we are team players and stated, "We will do whatever you think is the best for the school and the students."

They stated that they envisioned us teaching 5th Grade for the 2016-2017 school year. 4th grade for these learners was very unproductive academically and their behavior was out of control. They felt we could help get them back on track. The selling point was we were going to have three teachers, so our numbers were going to be extremely low compared to the 30 + students in most 5th grade classes throughout the district.

However, Debby had never taught anything above 3rd grade and I hadn't taught 5th Grade in five years. I had no desire to teach 5th Grade again. Unless I was to loop from second to fifth with my former students.

We went back and forth for some time. Fear of the unknown, and what if we fail? Debby expressed her concerns, "I'm not sure I can teach the 5th grade curriculum." My apprehension was expressed as "I've seen those students in assemblies, they are very ungrateful and disrespectful." Again, we wanted to do what was best for the school and students, and two people we respected thought we could do it. This went on for the rest of the day. Finally, Debby said, "Let's just do it." So we told our administration we would accept the challenge. We had the summer to figure it all out.

Being new parents we had no idea how much time would be involved in raising a baby. Summer flew by and we didn't really find any time to plan together or with our new colleague.

I did, however, get an opportunity to do some summer reading while the baby was napping. I read *The Innovator's Mindset* (George Couros), *Ditch That Textbook* (Matt Miller), *Launch* (John Spencer and AJ Juliani), and part of the *Mathematical Mindset* (Jo Boaler). Furthermore, since I was honored to be the 2016 PBS Digital Innovator for Nevada I earned a trip to Denver to attend a two day Digital Innovators workshop along with a day at the International Society for Technology in Education (ISTE) conference. I also become an avid Twitterer. I discovered that I wanted my experience in fifth grade to be a year of change and discovery. I wanted to try some new and innovative ideas. Somehow I convinced Debby to join me in this new venture.

Our first idea was flexible seating, and we decided to start with yoga balls. I mean, what's the worst that could happen? We fail and then get back up again? Next, we purchased a couple of futons and some gaming chairs. We also added some exercise equipment because we researched how students need to be active, and kinesthetic learning was a piece of the puzzle. Perhaps we were just trying to alleviate our fears of teaching 5th grade, but we were pretty intense about changing up our routines. We figured the physical appearance of the room was the easiest thing to change. For the first time my in my teaching career my classroom was full of color and other oddities. At that point I pondered whether I had lost my mind.

We knew our fellow 5th grade educator from last year. She taught 4th grade and we were pretty excited to be working with someone who was ready for a change. She agreed to try out flexible seating arrangement and added another perspective in our plan to incorporate some innovative ideas.

As we neared the start of the year fear set in. Debby and I must have looked like frazzled cartoon characters of our former selves. During the beginning of the year procedures, we had fellow educators ask on several occasions, "Are you feeling ok? You look pale!" and "Is the baby keeping you awake all night? Because you look tired." Furthermore, for those 5th grade teachers out there I'm sure you have heard this one, "Why would you choose 5th grade? God bless you, I couldn't do that. Those kids are so disrespectful." The knot in my stomach grew tighter, but we remained vigilant to make a difference and to have the best year possible.

The year started and I was amazed I only had 17 students. I had never had only 17 students; the lowest I had ever had was 20 in a second grade class and it was short-lived. So I felt blessed in that respect and felt it wouldn't last, but it did. If someone tells you class size doesn't matter, then they have been out of the classroom far too long. Maybe it doesn't matter looking at test data, but when you are creating a dynamic learning environment it makes a difference.

I am extremely grateful to our administration for giving us an opportunity to try some new ideas and for the low class sizes. Things were looking up, maybe the year wouldn't be so bad?

The mantra of Vicki Davis, The Cool Cat Teacher, was ringing in my head: "You have relate before you create. You have to relate before you create." When the students arrived the first thing we did was we initiated a social contract with the students. The students discussed and eventually agreed upon a set of norms in how to treat each other in the classroom. This was very self-empowering because the students discussed, agreed, and created the contract on their own. Their involvement to create a list of agreed upon norms - things like don't hit, stay on task, follow the Golden Rule, be respectful, and other important ideas of how to treat each other and the materials - gave them a feeling of ownership and responsibility. The mottos were, "Together we are one," and "If we believe, we will achieve."

This was our first of many creative and innovative ideas to help motivate the students to be lifelong learners and to make them feel in control of the learning process.

This year the learners have participated in a PBS commercial which is running on TV. They learned how many hours it takes to create a 30 second spot. The 5th grade students started their own Edcorps businesses. Each class had three different products to sell online and to the general public. Those items were school-made candles, bath bombs, sugar scrubs, and gardens in a jar. We were able to incorporate all curriculum areas in these business ventures.

Furthermore, students created Design Thinking projects which go a step beyond project based learning. Some of the designs they created were to build a school on Mars and invent a new sport. Our school was adopted by Mandalay Bay as a corporate sponsor, so a team of marketing students were able to visit the resort and experience the inner workings of a large corporation. We also incorporated robotics and coding during our weekly STEM Friday rotations. Students also became published authors by doing weekly blogging. Learners also experienced what it was like to be interviewed by newspapers. The learners have done some really amazing things this year, because we were allowed to take risks and think out of the box.

Furthermore, I have participated in many great opportunities to help change our climate and culture of the school into something amazing and things to help move our school forward as well. I talked in front of over 600 managers at Mandalay Bay in order promote our school. In essence, I have found my voice. I am the chair of our school organizational team which is our school's empowerment leadership team. I have published a few articles and am starting to find my voice as a writer along with many other amazing moments.

This year has been one of the most powerful teaching and learning experiences since I began 11 years ago. The key piece with our learners was creating those relationships in order to start off the year strong.

In my mind this has been truly the "best year ever." I met my fear head on and succeeded at more levels than I could have ever imagined. It made my classroom more dynamic, my students more empowered, and me a better educator.

Where has the time gone? It's May and I'm dreading the last day of school, fear is setting in, and once again I find myself in the principal's office having the conversation. "I will do whatever you think is in the best interest of the school moving forward." "We foresee you in a coaching mentor position; however, it's not set in stone." Consequently, I may be changing course in my educational endeavors next year. A lump in my throat, a knot in my stomach, and a sense of fear creeps in. "You mean not in a classroom? Will I become obsolete?" Fear settles in and, for a moment, pushes my best year ever aside. What will happen next? Only time will tell, but I know I will be ready for whatever opportunity and challenge lies ahead.

About Casey Korder

Casey Korder is a 5th grade educator at Parson Elementary School in Las Vegas, Nevada. This is his 11th year in education. He has as taught 2nd and 3rd grade too. He is the 2016 PBS Digital Learning Media Innovator and he has published several education articles online. When he is not inspiring students to be empowered lifelong learners he enjoys time with his wife and daughter, and playing ukulele. He writes a blog called Casey's Corner (rumblepups.wordpress.com). You may find him on Twitter @cjkorder.

Ways of Knowing

Urbie Delgado

Geez. 1000 words. That's the minimum I have to write for this piece. There was a time, long ago serving with the US Navy a thousand words was the briefest of sea stories. I'm older now. It seems I'm continuously pressed for time. So I'll be brief.

Four years ago I was in a rut. I mean it was a deep rut. My shtick was designing training. It was a 9 to 5 [the actual hours were 6:00 am to 3:00 pm] job. I thought it was important stuff. I did my best. At least I thought I did. It all changed when I had "the talk" with some trainees.

They clued me in. I talked to some more people. They filled in some more holes. I needed to make a change. I needed to. Actually, I didn't know what I needed to do. I was following the steps. The process to design effective training led me to this spot. So clearly I needed to go somewhere else for ideas on what to do next.

I turned to Google. I don't remember exactly what I typed in the search field. It didn't happen on the first try. I was at it for a while. That probably explains why I don't remember the search term. I do recall being a little upset because of a typo. Anyway, Google dutifully returned about 429,000 results (0.71 seconds) and the one on top was EdCampWestTexas. I didn't know what it was. So I clicked and read on. That was in August of 2013. The EdCamp was at the end of next month, September 28.

The experience changed my life. Professionally and personally I am a different person now. I [design] like a pirate. I flip the learning experience. I wasn't designing training anymore.

I was crafting experiences. Rather than read and click the learners I supported began learning by doing. "Never do anything for a learner the learner can do for themselves." I learned that while working toward my MS Ed. "Learned helplessness." I learned that from an Indiana teacher at an EdCamp in Texas.

I was off. I started crafting stories containing hooks. Andragogy calls that creating case studies. I like the pedagogy term more: stories and hooks. When I can I design authentic assessments that make the learning visible. Selecting the correct response from among several options, with a few distractors thrown in, doesn't work for me anymore. "How can I start a conversation between..." became my mantra.

The thing is, I'm not a teacher. I'm an instructional designer. More specifically, I'm a learning experience designer. EdCamps are a K-12 thing. Reflecting back on that first EdCamp makes me thankful they were so welcoming. I arrived late. It was a rainy Saturday. I walked up to the entrance of the Region 14 Education Service Center in Abilene, Texas a little anxious. I left on a sun shiny day [it was still raining but who cares] full of wonder and ideas. It was a 350 mile drive back to my place in Roswell, New Mexico. I don't remember the drive so much. The ideas I had are the ones I put into practice beginning the next workday.

I've been to some 50 or so more EdCamps since then. Each one introduces me to new people and their experiences. Each one deepens what I've learned from the ones that came before. Most of all I love the sharing. I love the diversity.

I'm not afraid. I mean I try things now. More things. Like at a conference for other designers in Las Vegas a few years ago I tried to use an activity I learned about at a CUE (Computer Using Educators) National Conference. It didn't work. I shared that out on some of the Twitter chats I participate in. I reflected on it. And when it finally dawned on me what went wrong I shared it out in a brief video. The old me, the pre EdCamp me, wouldn't have tried something new in front of his peers. If the old me had tried it he wouldn't have shared out the failure on social media. If the old me had shared it on social media he wouldn't be writing about it right now and linking to it.

There is more than one way of knowing. Learning stuff in school sets us off on a path. Workshops and conferences can build on what we know. It seems to me that too much of this leads us to a Tower of Babel kind of experience. In my case it led me to kind of forget why I was here. The learners I support matter more than the process of designing effective training. Design thinking, where the process begins with empathy, is something I am wholly committed to (I learned design thinking at EdCamp, too).

At every opportunity that I interact with my peers, with other designers, I share my EdCamp experiences. I have submitted conference proposals to several professional development groups serving designers and developers. Some have been accepted. I will continue doing so in the future. I see myself as a kind of trader. The EdCamps and other K-12 PD (Professional Development) activities I participate in have been in Washington, DC, Texas and California. Something I learned at EdCampIgnite in Escondido, California hadn't been heard before at EdCampPlano so I shared what I knew about it to get a conversation going. At EdCampFOMO just this past Saturday I shared an idea involving design thinking. It sent the conversation off on a tangent and ideas popped into heads and conversations diverged.

Anyway, ways of knowing. Let's keep mixing it up. Let's keep sharing what we know and how we know it. Nobody gets it right the first time every time.

About Urbie Delgado

Urbie Delgado is a learning experience designer. He holds an M.S.Ed. in instructional design. Urbie creates transformational learning experiences using design thinking and ADDIE (Analyze, Design, Develop, Implement, Evaluate) that engages learners. He has produced experiences for people in K-12, higher education, government and corporate organizations.

Connecting & Leading 'Naturally'

Summer Emens

Connecting, out on the open trail

Hike at Laguna Canyon, wildlife trail, Sunday, April 16, 2017

Connecting, out on the soccer field

I was cheering on my 6 year old girl from the sidelines as she played soccer. At that moment, I was "just mom." I loved being out there on the open field, soaking up the sun, and talking to the other mommies, forming a real connection, in real time.

I realized that being out on the field was not only good for the kids, it was good for us too. How we felt and connected made us better parents and role models for our children. The same has been true for me as an educator.

Connecting, out on the EDUfield playground.

Out on the open EDUfield playground, all are welcome. There is plenty of sun and open space. This is where we as educators can really make things happen: to promote change, innovate, grow, learn, play, connect, and lead, naturally.

The professional developments (PDs) I attended recently created a level playing field for educators to connect, but some still came with a clear advantage to contribute or lead 'naturally' due to their individual circumstances (the same is true with our students).

Some circumstances affecting participation and leadership opportunities were natural, such as proximity to an event. Some teachers had traveled further than others. I was fortunate in one aspect in that I did not have to travel very far to any of the PDs I attended locally.

Other circumstances that affected leadership opportunities appeared to be natural, but were artificially contrived by using district politics to promote some over others thru given directives, position or continuity in employment. An advantage was given to the educators who were supported by their district, to lead in their position. I was able to connect personally during the PDs I attended, and add value to the conversations that took place, but because I recently went thru something with my district, it made that, in itself, my Big Step.

Clearly, what was not on the level were leadership opportunities.

As educators, we tend to see individual circumstances as being personal issues our students face, but may be deeper rooted in socio-economic opportunity and other environmental or external factors. We stand up for our students, and create a culture and environment in our classrooms to allow all to exist and thrive. This is something far less talked about professionally.

So what can be done to promote equity in leadership?

First, it is important to understand how inequity happens or the way they do it (it's the wool over your eyes). How it happens isn't always clear cut, because there is no single way. So it's not always going to be seen or understood as being something targeted, or rooted in discrimination, because regardless of the underlying reasons of why it happens, the facts will usually appear completely mundane or have the usual elements of 'drama' to them as anything else in business and politics. It also appears to continue to be the status quo, uninterrupted, and not necessarily good for kids.

How inequity happens or the way they do it does not have a single formula- keep vigilant and on the lookout. Every story will be different. The tools or methods used to promote some, but not others will vary. Do your part to promote equity in leadership opportunities and stand up to district and administrative abuse of power that promote some over others to lead. If you stand by and let this happen and do nothing, it will become commonplace and will become the culture of the profession. There is a certain level of accountability we all share, yet clearly what promotes a culture of abuse is when those in a position to stop it, don't. They, the districts, are not above the law. I think this is how the union originally began- to prevent complete abuse of district power- but our K-12 public school system still seems to allow some teachers and TOSAs to exist but not others. I'm seeing a closed system that's fixed, where some are "allowed" and others "not allowed." So who's watching the district, its admin, and the union? The answer is that we should all be.

We are all leaders given the right conditions to participate. The "allowed" aren't the ones who lead better, they are the ones who have been given a platform. Opportunity should not be limited by a discriminating powerful source, allowing some, but not others to exist.

One antidote is to continue to provide professional developments that resemble an 'open field' and to embrace the 'no sage on the stage' rule, reducing favoritism through district politics. This doesn't seem to scream loud enough for me. Regardless of longevity in position or how awesome someone is, no one 'owns' a subject. If you are interested in a topic and want to be a lead but aren't as savvy as the next guy that the district politics has supported, do it anyway! It is possible to facilitate discussion without having to be the 'sage.'

The "rockstar" status given to some presenters during some PD's inadvertently contribute to the politics. For me, leadership is about making connections, and should never be that rigid. When I see it happening, it makes me wonder if this expertise is really 'worth the price.'

Of all the PDs I have recently attended, the 'unconferences' most resembled an 'open field' for me where everyone had an equal voice which allowed anyone to lead or participate according to the interests generated on that same day. No politics, established government, admin, principal, or other source, to stop it, or to segregate its teachers. They best promoted this with their rule, "NO SAGE ON THE STAGE."

The 'unconferences' I attended allowed equal opportunity for all to connect. Professionals came together with a common interest and created their agenda for that same day, with topics and leaders, but individual circumstances still affected leadership opportunity, 'naturally.'

About Summer Emens

Summer is "just a mom," a wife, and an educator. A few of her previous roles include STEM (math) TOSA, Math, STEAM and also Makerspace Teacher. She will be publishing a PIXEL ART MATH books, with a planned release of Fall 2017.

From Dream School to Action

Carla Meyrink

I never planned to become a teacher but about thirty years ago, it happened by happy accident. I moved to Santo Domingo and, in spite of the fact that I knew absolutely nothing about teaching, I was hired on as a middle school Language Arts teacher, simply because I spoke fluent English. I needed a job, so although I had no idea what getting into, I decided to give it a whirl... this seems to be an ongoing pattern in my life.

When I first started teaching in the Dominican Republic's hyper-traditional education system, my only real concern was trying to skirt the rules enough to help my students discover a love of reading and writing. I researched and experimented, trying out reading/writing workshop, and for years, that was enough — being able to give my students choice in the books they read, having animated discussions, making connections to their world, and teaching them to write creatively. I was on fire! I discovered that I loved teaching.

But all of that changed years later, when my son entered the first grade.

My happy little kindergartener, who couldn't wait to go to school every day (his backpack was by the door, ready to go, before I even got out of the shower), suddenly morphed into a child I didn't recognize. He complained about how bored he was, refused to go to school in the morning, and cried over his dull, endless homework. The learning was rote memorization and I cringed as I helped him memorize facts for his tests. My daughter was still enjoying learning through play at preschool, but it wouldn't be long until she was also in elementary. I had two curious kids who loved to discover the world, and I couldn't imagine them spending twelve years copying words off of a whiteboard. My friends also had young children who were facing the same bleak future. Something had to give.

I had become friends with a group of teachers who were also passionate about their work and eager to experiment with new teaching techniques. We'd meet on weekends for breakfast to share our ideas, complain about our schools (which were incredibly traditional), laugh about the latest exploits of our students, complain about our schools, plan playdates for our children, and… complain some more about our schools. We could identify the problems we faced and come up with solutions, but we were powerless to implement them.

One day at our weekend breakfast, tired of whining about things I couldn't control, I blurted out, "Why don't we open our own school?"

There was dead silence around the table. No one was going there.

But then the ever-positive, Tami said, "Sure, let's do it. It'll be fun." For years, we laughed over that naive idea — "It'll be fun." We had no idea what we were getting into…

So we did it. The two of us devoted the next year to hammering out our philosophy. We spent hours dreaming of the ideal school — and planning how to make it a reality. We read Punished by Rewards by Alfie Kohn, and his ideas became the bedrock of our school. There would be no punishments and no rewards. No honor roll, no grades, no detentions. We wanted small class sizes, no textbooks but lots of real books, and hands-on, integrated learning that would empower our students.

It was also important to us to keep our prices as low as we could. The Dominican Republic has a very weak public education system, so in order to educate their children, parents have to put them in private schools, which many can't afford. We wanted to create a strong school that could serve a struggling middle class.

As with many new project ideas, money was a problem. We were almost forced to quit before we'd even begun, because we had no savings and finding seed money was much harder than we'd expected. But just when we'd decided to give up, our friend Lynn miraculously decided to jump on board. She invested in the school, which meant we could finally take our first concrete steps towards creating it. We found a small house to rent and somehow convinced eight families to take the risk of putting their children in our school-that-didn't-yet-exist. We had to figure out how to run a business, what the laws were for starting a school, and try to assure the Ministry of Education that we could do this. It was terrifying.

When you decide to undertake this kind of adventure, it's scary and you need a cheerleader. During the day, I had my business partner and friends to dream with, but in the evenings I was an anxious mess. One day, I told my husband that I was going to abandon the idea. When he asked me why, I said, "It's just too much. What if it doesn't work out? What if we fail?"

"Well," he said, "What have you got to lose? If you don't try, then you'll fail for sure. And you'll always wonder what could have happened. If you try and it doesn't work, at least you'll have the satisfaction of knowing you gave it a shot."

Those were exactly the words I needed to hear. We found a house to rent in the summer of 1998 and got to work. We cleaned, painted, found second-hand furniture, raided our kids' bookshelves for our classroom libraries, and made everything we could by hand. When we opened the doors to our 11 first through third grade students in September, it was the strangest little homemade school, but we couldn't have felt any prouder.

We taught with big books, manipulatives, and hands-on projects. We researched and built our curriculum, integrating the subject areas as much as possible. That September, Hurricane Georges made a direct hit on Santo Domingo – for months the city was a mess and we had no electricity – but we saw it as an opportunity and by integrating it into our projects, it became a great learning experience. After that, every hurdle we encountered, every social issue the country faced, became another way to teach our kids about life and problem solving.

Those first few years were hard. We offered after-school art classes, tutoring, and English classes in order to pay our bills and our tiny staff. We met with potential parents and celebrated every time someone enrolled a child. We rented slightly bigger houses to accommodate our slowly growing school and we fought battles with the Ministry of Education over our teaching methodology. We struggled to hire teachers who were a bit skeptical about teaching in the bedrooms of small houses. But, amazingly, some of them joined us: passionate educators who were willing to work long hours for little pay. We were sued by neighbours who didn't want a school in their neighbourhood and weathered hyperinflation under a failing government.

Now, 19 years later, we own our own land and we're building the school of our dreams. We're accredited in both the Dominican Republic and the U.S. We have over 400 students and we're about to celebrate our 10th graduation. We started the school for our own children — all of whom graduated years ago

— and now, we not only continue it for all of our students but also in the hope that we can have a positive impact on a country we love.

It's been quite a ride. Every once in a while, I look around our campus and feel overwhelming gratitude. We have an incredible staff – passionate, innovative teachers who share a common vision. Our teachers are a close-knit community of risk-takers who know the power of a dream. We're also lucky to have supportive families who believe in us and who were willing to take a bet on our vision when we were just a handful of people in a house-turned-school. And, best of all, we have students who love coming to school in the morning.

My husband was right: if you have a dream you've been holding onto, go for it! Give it a try. If you don't, you'll never know what could have happened. And if you do... well, sometimes dreams come true.

About Carla Meyrink

Originally from Vancouver, Canada, Carla moved to the Dominican Republic about 30 years ago where she taught middle school and secondary Language Arts. She co-founded The Community for Learning in 1998 and has been experimenting in education ever since. She blogs at:

146

http://teachingexperiment.com/

and loves to connect with teachers on Twitter @carlameyrink

Working Relationships

I'm not the smartest fellow in the world, but I can sure pick smart colleagues.
- Franklin D. Roosevelt

Team Stripes

Kelly Nunes

Let's face it, it can be quite difficult finding "your place" in your school or workplace. In my experience through 15 years in education, I've seen it go down in one of two ways. Way number one: you're a new teacher, excited, pumped, ready to learn and share. Then cue in the department or grade level that frankly can be "difficult." Finding a balance between being new and "taking a back seat" and yet not getting walked on in order to share your great ideas is quite the mystery. Way number two: you automatically find THAT person who you just click with. The person who helps keep your sanity, has similar goals and interests, and above all is just amazing and accepts you for your flaws.

I was probably at the most trying and difficult time in my career. Just a year of constant challenge and my confidence was diminishing in my position at my job. Then truly, this young (like 8 years younger than me), beautiful woman was hired in a similar position as myself. It was then I found "MY" person. She was finding her way in a job with duties she was not yet accustomed to. Whereas, I had the experience of the position and was excited for her enthusiasm and ideas. It also helped that we almost instantly connected on a personal level of building a friendship. Our sarcasm is similar, we are optimists at heart, fear failure, and above all want to make a darn difference!

What solidified our relationship was our goals! #wegotgoals We both were determined and passionate about doing good and going beyond just our district. We attended an EdTechTeam

Summit and the inspiration came...let's do it! We WANT to be part of this great environment. Seriously, if you've ever attended a EdTechTeam Summit you understand our excitement. Educators WANT to learn, educators are coming together to better themselves, educators are EXCITED! It is a weekend full of brain-busting implementation ideas in every educational format you can think of. But most of all: It. Is. FUN! It sucks you in...it reignites a fire to be...BETTER! So, from there on out it was our goal to present and potentially become part of this "team."

Our first time presenting at a Summit was for our local district. Yes, we planned to wear our matching EdTechTeam t-shirts, because we are cool like that- hehe! Then, we applied and were accepted to present that required us to travel a little further. Without planning, without talking about it; it began...we were up at the crack of dawn in order to arrive on time and we saw each other...STRIPES! We had both decided to wear black and gray stripes. Too late to change...we were going with it. Upon arriving we took our picture at the photo booth and an amazing, energetic woman professed loudly, "Oh my goodness...Team Stripes!" #teamstripes was born!

To say the least, through this bond we stick together through hardship, challenges, excitement, and success. We continue to work on our goals and push each other! We have met amazing people, who quite frankly have been initiated by coincidently wearing "stripes" to be part of the "team." Our team. Not our team in a possessive way, but a collective way. A group of people that collaborate, work together, share similar goals, and above all else have fun! Fun, I think, is overlooked, yet soooo essential. Along with the fact that we are us…we are individuals who do not lose who we are, nor try to be like anyone else. We support one another even if feedback and improvement is needed. We absolutely LOVE to stereotypically, "make a difference." We LOVE to be able to work together to support and help other educators reach their potential and just. Be. Better!

So, here it is: Find your "person." This job can be tough enough with expectations and requirements. Find your person who will laugh with you, cry (seriously) with you, has similar goals, will give you feedback (everyone is a learner and could always use it), but above all else let's you be YOU! I laugh, but seriously my husband, as much as he is my world and rock, does not quite understand everything there is about my profession that having my Team Stripe, soul sister has been a Godsend. I am a BETTER educator for that. I am a BETTER person for that! I am truly blessed and only hope you will be too!

About Kelly Nunes

Kelly is an instructional coach with a focus on English Learners for Hesperia Unified School District servicing grades TK-12. She also enjoys presenting at conferences & EdTechTeam Summits. Being a Google Certified Educator &

Trainer brings her excitement for innovation and collaboration! She aspires to always get "Googley!" She is passionate that you should, "Treat people as if they were what they ought to be and you help them become what they are capable of becoming." - Goethe

Twitter:@elcoachkelly

Website: bit.ly/educ82learn

Down the Twitter Rabbit Hole

Meagan Kelly

The Why

A year ago, I began to feel isolated as a teacher within my school site. It's hard to say the exact reason for this feeling of isolation. Most likely, it had to do with the number of responsibilities that I had on my plate that drew me into several different departments. Now, don't get me wrong - I do not regret any of these opportunities or challenges. In fact, I have found myself growing as an educator and leader due to these responsibilities. However, by being pulled in multiple directions, it was easy to feel isolated since I was not completely connected with any one department.

Although isolation can be debilitating as a teacher, it is also a choice. As educators living in the 21st century, we have the unique ability to communicate and collaborate with other educators around the world through Twitter, email, blogs, Google Hangouts, and much more. There are thousands of teachers that are ready to connect and grow professionally with you. They share the same passion for learning and excitement about education. They have ideas and resources that they want to share and develop.

Choose to connect. Develop a Professional Learning Network (PLN). Find other educators like you - educators that are excited to grow and share resources to support student learning. It's not just good for you but it is good for your students.

For myself, Twitter allowed me to connect with dozens of educators, within and outside of my district, that have had a profound affect upon myself as a teacher which, in turn, has had a positive impact on student learning in my classroom.

I want to share with you how I fell down the "Twitter Rabbit Hole"...

My Introduction to Twitter

The first time I heard about Twitter for professional development was several years ago as I attended my first EdTechTeam Summit. At the time, I was completing my master's degree in Educational Leadership, so professional development was a part of my everyday life. I started my Twitter account, posted about half a dozen times, and only returned to it sporadically over the next several years. Honestly, I think that the combination of my regular duties as a teacher, graduate student, and coordinator of several on-campus programs was enough to cause me to lose some interest in seeking out my own professional development. I knew that Twitter was beneficial for professional development as a teacher, but I had found myself busy with so many things that the idea of using Twitter was pushed aside.

The second time that I realized Twitter could be a great professional development tool was during our book club meeting, where we were reading *Kids Deserve It* by Adam Welcome and Todd Nesloney. Chapter 2 of the book is titled "Don't Live on an Island" which is an incredibly important topic in education. In the book, they write:

"Whatever the reason for the isolation, if you want to create that spark, you have to 'get off the island' and start collaborating. The good news is you

can choose whom to connect and collaborate with – and they don't have to be within the walls of your building."

I'm not sure what it was about this quote, but it really struck a chord with me. It's not so much that I have not had the opportunity to collaborate. That isn't it at all. Instead, the idea that really hit me was that collaboration can extend far beyond the walls of your classroom or the gate of your school. As someone who deems herself to be fairly tech savvy, I find myself disappointed that this thought never occurred to me. How did I not realize that collaboration amongst teachers could done through social media? Or, better question…Did I know this and I was too afraid to take the jump, to take the risk? Quite frankly, it is a bit terrifying. The idea of writing and putting your thoughts into physical words can be very intimidating. After all, what if someone doesn't like what you have written? What if they think that you are just trying to show off? What if no one cares?

The authors continue to write:

"So, I began to connect with others, share my ideas, and even collaborate! When I began my teaching career, I never imagined I'd work with people from all over the world. But my connections via Twitter have led to opportunities for my students and me to work with students in other countries, Olympic and Paralympic athletes, White House personnel, and so many others."

Doesn't that sound amazing? I think so!

The third time I realized Twitter could be used as professional development was when I attended the EdTechTeam Summit within my own district. Everyone was using Twitter! I even attended a "Twitter Chat Live" session that discussed joining online chats on education. Apparently, there are ton of these chats on Twitter all the time! So, I made the decision that I needed to use Twitter as a professional development resource. I had found myself with a great desire for more professional development and to participate in discussions with other educators. However, this was not only for myself, but for the growth and success of my own students. The only way that they can grow and succeed is if I am willing to do the same.

Down the Twitter Rabbit Hole

I'll be honest... I fell hard for Twitter. I fell down this rabbit hole of following educators, reading blogs, sharing my own resource, and communicating with educators around the world.

To begin, I created a few challenges for myself: 1.) Join a Twitter Chat, 2.) Develop a Professional Learning Network (PLN)of educators, and 3.) Blog weekly and share posts via Twitter.

Joining a "live" Twitter chat was one of the first things that I did when I became involved with Twitter. Honestly, it was very intimidating. These chats moved so quickly that I found it difficult to keep up with all of the conversations that were occurring within the hour-long window of time. However, it was completely exhilarating. I found it to be exciting to have conversation with teachers all over the world who were dedicated to improving their teaching practices and trying new things in their classroom - all to support their students.

In addition to this, I also had a fledgling blog that I had created (www.i-heart-edu.com) but had spent little time developing or writing. One of my goals was to blog every week and share my ideas and thoughts with other educators. Although very few people read my blog in the beginning, it was still a great time to reflect on my practices. Eventually, other educators began sharing my blog posts on Twitter and I started participating in amazing conversations across the world. As an example, I am currently planning a Statistical Research Project with a teacher from Brazil where the students will complete a survey and analyze the results from their different environments. The possibilities are endless!

By joining Twitter and blogging weekly, I quickly connected with many amazing educators, as well as teachers within my own district. These individuals have encouraged me and helped to grow in more ways than they realize. They have been a source of encouragement, inspiration, knowledge, and strength. I have tried so many new things in my classroom with my students due to these educators. Personally, I thought that these people did not exist until I joined Twitter but I am not sure where I would be without them.

Profound Impacts

Twitter has had an enormous and profound impact upon my personal and professional life due the educators that I have followed, talked to, and collaborated with throughout the last school year.

Here are just a few ways these individuals have shaped my personal and professional life:

- I have a group of teachers that I can talk to when I need anything - ideas, advice, inspiration, etc. I have made connections with teachers all over the United States but, also, all over the world.
- I have brought new ideas into my classroom and into our school, such as Breakout EDU, 20Time Projects, HyperDocs, and other resources that engage and excite students in their learning process.

- I have had the opportunity to participate in conferences and summits to share educational technology resources. Although I love sharing resources and training teachers, the conversations that I have with these teachers always spark new ideas for my classroom.
- Our district has started our own District Twitter Chat (#HUSDChat) which has created collaboration and opened conversation across our sites. It is easy to feel isolated at our own sites; however, some of my best personal and professional relationships have been formed with teachers that are not at my school site.
- Through the support of these educators, I have been pushed outside of my comfort zone to apply to programs such as the Google for Education Trainer and Innovator programs, which has opened amazing opportunities to support teachers and students.

All of these things have occurred due to the educators I have connected with on Twitter. Although I would love to name all these educators, there are just too many amazing people to mention but they know who they are because of the conversations we have had over the last year.

Remember this - isolation and loneliness is a choice in education. Don't allow yourself to be isolated and disconnected. It isn't good for you, so it isn't good for your students.

Join Twitter. Blog regularly. Develop your PLN. Grow.

About Meagan Kelly

Meagan Kelly is a Google for Education Certified Trainer and Innovator from Hesperia California. She is currently a middle school Math and AVID teacher, as well as the Team Technology Leader and AVID coordinator.

Twitter: @meagan_e_kelly

Website: www.i-heart-edu.com

Why Induction Programs are Broken (and how to fix them!)

DJ Latcham

Congratulations! You just obtained your teaching credential, passed all your required examinations, paid your necessary fees, and now you have found your first teaching position. Accomplishing just one of these feats is a great victory, but as a teacher, you will be asked to continuously do more with less, so it's better you get used to that now rather than later in your career.

There are very few moments more exciting than the moment you are handed the keys to your first ever classroom. The years of anticipation, planning, and dreaming all coincide with feelings of anxiety as the weight of your decisions slowly enter your mind. You envision how you will set up the space, the faces of your students, and where your much needed coffee pot will go for those early mornings and late nights that are ahead of you.

Most beginning teachers are not aware of the harsh reality that the first year of teaching often becomes. Despite the excitement and joy of having your own classroom, the steep learning curve and responsibilities put on new teachers can often be strangling, even for the most prepared educators. I began my career as an elementary teacher in a 6th grade classroom at a very underprivileged school in Sacramento, CA. I had no clue the level of commitment I would have to make to my students, career, and myself that first year. And then I found out I had to complete my mandated beginning teacher induction program...

Teacher Induction Programs are designed to ensure new teachers are adequately prepared and supported throughout their beginning years of teaching. In California, the Commission on Teacher Credentialing mandates that all teachers go through a two year program where new teachers are paired with an experienced teacher, called a support provider, as they work on perfecting the art of teaching. In Star Wars terms, you are the young padawan under the tutelage of the Jedi Knight, in hopes of one day becoming a Jedi Master in the teaching world.

Unfortunately, teacher induction programs are broken and do not work as they should. Despite best intentions, induction programs often fail at the one aspect they are intended to provide: support for new teachers. Instead of helping to prepare new teachers, they add more work that does not improve teaching pedagogy. Rather than mentoring new teachers on classroom management and relationship building (two enormously overlooked aspects of credentialing programs), induction programs choose to focus on reflection strategies. Between the long hours of preparation and actual teaching, I was barely managing to deliver my curriculum every day, let alone reflect on my teaching and learn from my mistakes! Induction programs often connect people in spite of teaching, rather than because of it, which needs to change.

So do we need induction programs at all? And if so, how do we make them relevant to new teachers?

Yes, I believe that induction programs are still needed and can be useful for new teachers, but not in the current form. Teaching is tough and can be extremely difficult if you are not in the most supportive environment. I was extremely fortunate my first year as I was placed at a site with experienced teachers who went out of their way to help support and guide me as I struggled to find my way as a new teacher. Between pedagogy discussions, curriculum design, and trusted techniques, I was given a more structured support network than any induction program could provide. I am aware enough that this will not and may never occur for some teachers, but elements can be used to create a design that does work.

Step 1: Create meaningful connections between new and experienced teachers. The research is clear: students learn better from teachers they are able to make relationships with, why would teacher mentorships be any different. The idea that you can pair a brand new teacher with a veteran educator and assume it will be beneficial simply because they both work in the same district is about as smart as the concept that all students will enjoy their classmates because they share the same teacher! More concerted efforts should be made to pair teachers and mentors together based on similarities and relationships that can be more impactful for both parties, and ultimately have a greater effect on teaching practices.

Step 2: Focus induction programs on meaningful professional development to the teacher. After years of throwing canned in-service programs at teachers hoping one would stick, education as a discipline is finally coming around to the idea that teacher professional development is not a one size fits all concept. Why should induction programs be any different? By offering an array of professional development options that is focused on the most relevant needs, beginning teachers are able to actively monitor their own strengths and targeted areas of growth as they look to better their craft.

Step 3: Concentrate on reducing teacher burden making the work relevant. Teachers are the worst students in the world. Ask any person who has ever taught to a room full of teachers. One reason is that teachers can spot meaningless assignments better than anyone and don't find value in tasks that are not relevant to them. Traditional induction programs make assignments so far removed from the actual teaching practice in the classroom that teachers often write them off or find them invaluable. Induction programs should be tailored to helping new teachers in their classrooms specifically and increase the likelihood of success for the future as well as the present.

Hopefully by following the above steps, new teachers can feel supported and have a better experience as they set out to become the Jedi Masters of Education. At the very least, perhaps we should start carrying light sabers to prove a point.

About DJ Latcham

DJ is an educator in Sacramento, CA to a wild bunch of awesome middle school students. Latcham teaches English and History, or as he says: "the story of how stuff happened, how it affected others, and why we should care." Find him on twitter: @mrlatcham

Find YOUR Tribe

Cori Orlando

Find YOUR People

I have been out of the classroom and work as a "coach" now at the district level for three years. When I was in the classroom, I did not understand the power and impact of collaboration. I planned with partners, we hung out during non school hours, but I now have a different perspective on "collaboration". To me, there are two different, yet similar types of collaboration.

#tribematters: This idea of finding your tribe is new to me...but so transformative! It wasn't until this last year that I feel I have found my tribe people and understood the impact. I describe a tribe as a group of YOUR people. These are the people that "get" you. They understand where you are coming from, understand where you want to go and help you to get there. They are there to listen when you need an ear, lift you when you are down, celebrate when there are wins and push you farther than you thought you could go. Your tribe members don't necessarily need to be like-minded people, but they are usually like-hearted people...that is where the connection is made.

I personally have been extremely blessed to have found my tribe! It is not large, but they are large in my life. It is made up of amazing, humble educational leaders with hearts of gold. It is interesting because some of them don't even know each other...yet. Some of them do know each other, but are just figuring out their connection to me. Regardless...I would not have survived this last year without this crew!

There have been many times of self doubt, pitfalls, frustration, small wins, big wins, naysaying, bullying, good times and bad...and they have seen me through them all. They have helped me to see things and believe things in myself that I never knew. They put me in check when needed and they absolutely stretch me AND my thinking.

I have come to rely on this amazing group of people for a lot. I just hope that I can give back in return. This should be a two way street and I often wonder if I am pulling my weight in these relationships. I often reflect and wonder how I can give back to them. I don't feel I much to give, besides my ear and my heart...both of those are always free and clear when/if they are needed...I hope they know that.

#bettertogether: I have come to REALLY understand and promote this one! No longer can we, as educators, live in silos. It is not fair to ourselves or those around us. There is so much great out there; it needs to be shared.

I know that no educational idea or activity of mine is an original. I take things that are shared and I tweak them to make them work for me or my situation. We should all be doing this. As educators, we are working so hard on our own, but it doesn't have to be that way. I have witnessed the power of collaboration and it needs to be happening...plain and simple. I have personally witnessed the power of people collaborating and the payoff is immense!

Through the power of social media (Twitter especially) we have a wealth of information right at our fingertips. We must tap into that. I have grown by leaps and bounds from participating in Twitter chats and following amazing people. The educational Twitter community is amazing! Walls are flattened and it is a sharing fest. It is definitely a culture of #shareforward. People learn from others, and then share their twist or their take and share that with others and it goes on and on. Here is the other powerful piece...the magic is what happens beyond the 140 characters. I will tell you...EVERY SINGLE person in my tribe, started with a Twitter connection. I don't really know how it happened, it just did. These people that were strangers to me a year ago, I now can call my friends. It is pretty mind blowing.

As much as I love these connections with people that are not local to me, there is something to be said with local collaboration! I believe it is so important for educators to be collaborating across classrooms, grade levels, sites, roles, districts, counties...I have seen the power that comes from this. It is so important to learn from those who can bring a different perspective.

Just this week, I witnessed something incredible with educators in our district. One person gave a "shoutout" on Twitter about someone (from a different school site) helping them learn something new. The next thing I know, there is another tweet of that person #sharingforward. Then there was a third tweet was that person then #sharingforward BUT with a twist...SHE then learned something new from the person she was helping. The beauty...these were people from three different sites,three different grades and two different roles.

Another avenue that creates this #bettertogether culture is #EdCamps or meet-ups. These provide time, space and opportunities for people to gather and discuss education. I have seen many people make connections with others and collaborate with people whom they would never have met otherwise. THAT is powerful!

I am so grateful for the people and opportunities that I have had because of relationships that have been built through these connections. Not to mention the huge growth that has occurred. I urge you to reach out to find YOUR people and cherish them.

About Cori Orlando

Cori Orlando is a K-4 teacher for 14 years who is currently a TOSA (teacher on special assignment) in Simi Valley USD. Through her belief in #failforward, she encourages others to step outside of their comfort zone and #riskforward. Cori is a Google Certified Educator Level 1 and 2 and helps run #SVTChat.

Blog Site: http://leadinginlimbo.weebly.com/
Twitter: @coriorlando1
Email: cori.orlando@simivalleyusd.org

Every Day is an Adventure

It's a dangerous business, Frodo, going out your door. You step onto the road, and if you don't keep your feet, there's no knowing where you might be swept off to.

– Bilbo Baggins, *The Lord of the Rings*

The Best Year: How 10 Dollars Left in My PD Budget Changed My Life

Carlos Galvez

I'm a PE teacher. You know, the one that all the kids in school know and love to say hello to in the hallways. To be honest, I wouldn't be a teacher of any other subject. I love what I do and I love to be able to impact my students with not just teaching them how to be healthy but to hopefully one day be able to make new friends when someone asks, "Hey, wanna play ultimate frisbee with us tomorrow?" and for them to say "Absolutely!" I try to make sure my students are learning how sports are played. Not necessarily that you have to be the person who scores all the goals in a soccer match but that it's more important to know how and why that goal was scored. This is a belief I've always had as an educator.

I'm pretty sure you have come out of a PD conference saying to yourself "I didn't learn many new things this time." Well, PE conferences are not very different. In fact, because we have sports backgrounds, PE teachers tend to go to conferences just to tell people how they can do things better than you. I believe it goes like this: "And this is the way we do Dynamic Stretching at our school" and me, in my head thinking, "I've been doing it this way for 4 years…." After attending a couple of conferences where unfortunately I didn't feel that I got as much as I wanted from them I promised myself that I would use my school's PD funds in a smarter way. This is where my journey began.

I started by doing some reflecting and finding some areas for improvement. Then I decided that going the certification route instead of the conference route would be more beneficial for my students. It would allow me learn from the best instructors in the world and learn all the nooks and crannies of the sport I in which I wanted to get certified. So after doing some research I decided to go for a Level 1 tennis coach and a Level 1 swimming coach. Both of these sports were sports I was a good athlete at but I lacked instructional knowledge. Long story short I had obtained both certifications by January of that school year. Both certifications were 3 days long, had practice teaching and exams and required my full attention but in the end I walked (maybe limped) out of there with a globally recognised level 1 certification in swimming and tennis. A couple of days later I began a Net Unit with my students in PE and I was amazed at how I was picking up errors with grip, swing, footwork, etc. My students benefited greatly from my newfound expertise in tennis.

With $10 left in my PD budget I set out to possibly find a free certification so I could say that I got 3 that year. This proved difficult as the big sports federations tend to charge money. Then I remembered about a friend of mine who said she had obtained a Google Educator Certification. So I went on bing.com and googled it. Haha! Just kidding I googled it on Google. Suddenly there it was. Staring right at me. Google Educator Level 1..... $10. And I could do the training modules myself? Before I knew it I was 2 units in. I may have forgotten to mention that I live in China. Google is blocked in China and we have big issues with its use. I decided to still go for it. After all, that yellow badge would look good on my resume. 4 or 5 weeks later I take the 3 hour test and passed it. By the time I came back from the bathroom from sitting there for 3 hours I had gotten notifications on every device I own. The badge was already in my inbox waiting for me. I was so proud. My wife, who has been my number one fan, was so excited. 3 certifications in one year.

Coming into work on the Monday I looked at my brand new Google Educator badge and thought to myself, if level 1 was $10 then how much is level 2? $30? So I went for it! Something weird was happening to me though. I was beginning to apply Google Apps aka GAFE in my PE classes. I began using Google Forms for my students to teach themselves dance choreographies and to track their fitness results. I began using PBL in my health classes and began to use Hyperdocs. Was I applying the things that I was learning into my classes that quickly? Yes. As I was studying for level 2 I was starting to become more practical when planning my classes, to collaborate with teachers and assessing students. I found myself printing a lot less and even if I didn't always use Google Apps, I was saving lots of time. Wanna know the truth? I failed my level 2 test but because I had detected some discrepancies with the test, Google gave me a voucher to retake the test. This was good because this time I was able to know the size of the beast that I had to defeat. 2 weeks later there I was, staring at my level 2 certification. So proud of myself. But wait, there was a post on my Google+ groups that said. You can now apply for the Google Certified Innovators program!

The application was long. Really long. I was asked to submit a project or proposal that I was doing at the time that could "change education." You know, like the ones we do all the time? The other problem was that I had about 10 days to do it. At the time I had been working with some students on a dance project which ended up turning into what I call No Passion Left Behind.

My project helps to ensure that teachers are going the extra mile to help students find their passions early on. I had started this project way before I even knew about Google for Education so this was my only hope. I filled in the application, created a slide deck, made a quick 2 minute video and pressed submit.... Email from Google. Subject: Congratulations Carlos. Welcome to the Google Certified Innovators Program. Are you kidding me? I'm going to Google this summer?

Walking into Google in Boulder, Colorado gave me chills. It was like Charlie and the Chocolate Factory. Me along 35 other teachers, tech integrators and even vice-principals could not believe it. This was my journey. But what about theirs? How were they seeking to change education? 3 days at Google and working with the Google for Education team along with the EdtechTeam transformed me. We were encouraged and given tips on how to carry out our projects to completion. We were given motivational speeches to not be afraid to fail. We learned how Google approaches staff retention and what being "Googley" means. The most amazing thing that came out of those three days was the people I met. My cohort, our coaches, our leaders and organizers all came together to create magic. But this was not a trick. It was transformation. We now belong to a special group, all of whom are seeking change and innovation in education. We are the #GoogleEI.

5 certifications in one year. Oh yeah, I forgot to mention another one. Father. My beautiful wife Cecilia and I had our boy right around the time all this was happening. Lucca is a healthy baby. He's a happy baby. One day I will tell him about the year he was born. I'll make sure he know's how important it is to put your students first if he decides to become a teacher. I'll make

sure he knows that it's okay to hack and disrupt learning. Because this is all bigger than us. All we can do is make sure our students are getting the best version of ourselves every time we walk into that classroom. That we are prepared to take our students to the next level. After all, we made the choice to be here.

About Carlos Galvez

Carlos began in education back in the late 90's when his mother convinced him to become an English teacher in Guatemala. Since then his career has taken him to Italy and now China as he found a passion for Physical Education later in life. In his career at Shekou International School he's been able to incorporate technology with the philosophy that it's not a replacement for teaching, but an added value to understanding. Carlos is a Google Google Certified Innovator and Certified Trainer and has a passion for passion projects.

We All Fall Down

Brian Costello

Teaching is incredibly difficult. As a profession it often has the ability to either galvanize people or destroy them. In the course of a given day, you can be asked to play roles that vary from therapist, to educator, to a child's sole source of food or clothing for a day. Every educator is asked to make thousands of decisions daily. Each one of those decisions is made, not in a vacuum, but in the extreme interconnected web of a classroom or school environment. That crucible is not what makes the profession so taxing. Instead, it is the simple fact that education is a personal profession. As an educator, my personal relationships with students, staff, and families in the community are a major part of being successful. That also means that it is extremely challenging for educators to "leave it at work". It is incredibly difficult to act as a caregiver, friend, support system, and more for so many children and disconnect from that each day. Each time we play a role in another chapter of a child's story is a deeply personal moment. I thought of many of those chapters, many of those moments, to share. But, those are their stories. This one is uniquely mine:

Everything was perfect. I was going into my fifth year of teaching I knew what I was doing. I had just finished a year as my district's teacher of the year and two excellent years of teaching. That year was my second school year as a father, as a full time graduate student in administration, and my second full classroom year as an avid user of Twitter. Why does that matter? Simply put, with over a year of these experiences, I wasn't very good at figuring out how it all fit. I had tried everything, but I for a while I had struggled to understand how to harness all the new knowledge.

It was also the first full year with my new Chief School Administrator. My previous CSA was the person who had given me a chance as an educator. She had given me an opportunity and trusted me to succeed within that role. Over the previous four years I had developed confidence, and a reason for confidence. I was eager to be a part of the change process with our new administrator and to impress upon him how fantastic I was as an educator. Unfortunately, I was wrong. Twitter had taught me so many new things. I wanted to implement them all. Being a father had placed in me a new sense of empathy. All of which should have made me better. Instead, those things combined to make my classroom slightly chaotic and my teaching less effective. I was just starting to reinvent myself as an educator, to understand how all of these new pieces fit to make me better. I recognized my strengths, my weaknesses, and how I could leverage both to make my students better. The process was slow, a little painful, and humbling. I needed the experience and I came to understand myself and my profession much better.

One thing I did have, was an incredible classroom redesign. I didn't get to fully complete the new environment because of construction at our school leaving me with only 48 hours to create a new space. I had spent two straight days, about 20 hours, working on my classroom redesign. Creating a space with alternative seating, table arrangements, and gave every area of the room a purpose. It could have used another 20 hours. Regardless, it was something I took pride in, and something my students loved.

That year started well enough. What I didn't realize was the poor impression I had made in the half year previous left me in a serious deficit with my new administrator. I was starting to get a handle on how everything fit. My empathy as a father, my incredible learning from my new network of educators, and my kids were all finally starting to fit. I was learning how to correct mistakes I had made in the past and realized how far off I was in the previous year. I learned humility, dedication, and resilience. Finally, it was all starting to click. Then, it wasn't.

In December of that year, with little to no support, I found myself in one of the most stressful and disheartening situations of my career. It was personal. It was about the thing I was most proud of for that year. I was improving my organization, but the reality was I needed time to create the organizational structure. That time didn't exist in the beginning of the year due to construction. Once the kids were there every day, I was fortunate to hold onto the structures I had developed thus far. At times I wavered from reasonable to moderately disorganized. With lots of projects, major family events, and a pair of final interviews for administration jobs that simply didn't materialize, it was an extremely hectic time and unsurprisingly my classroom organization mirrored that. It wasn't awful, but I remember leaving some things in disarray on a Friday, knowing I would have to do some organization on the following Monday morning.

I walked in on that Monday morning, unsuspecting of the personal soul crushing I was about to endure. My CSA asked to see me before I had made it to my classroom. He proceeded to tell me that my classroom was not a learning environment. I was hoping to have time to improve the organizing structures in my classroom, instead I was told I was losing my class. That Friday I would be without my kids. I would have to plan for them to be with a substitute in our Library. On that day another teacher would be redesigning my classroom and I would be there to help. The things I valued most in my classroom design were being taken from me. My class was going to be with a sub for the day while I had a friend and colleague change everything I had worked so hard to create.

That Friday I swallowed my pride. It was one of the hardest things I had ever done as a professional. If not for the support of a few close mentors I am not sure how I would have moved forward. I spent a day taking apart everything I believed was right in my classroom and the rest of that year living in someone else's home. It is the equivalent of living out of a hotel room. Sure, it looks nice, it may even be extremely functional, but it isn't your own. As I had mentioned before, teaching is a personal profession. Everything about my classroom design was personal for me. I cared deeply about providing a special space for my kids to learn. One that was reactive to their needs. Time, money, and most importantly my heart was invested in creating that space. In one Friday in December, it was gone. I still have a lot of the materials in my garage. It may seem like an overreaction, but a piece of me was destroyed when that classroom was taken from me and my kids.

There has never been a more powerful defining moment in my career. I have been through so many ups and downs in my career, but no point lower. I had a choice: be better or give up. In that moment I chose to persevere. I have improved, learned, and worked to stay out of that place. That was an incredibly difficult place. I struggled through the next few months. While I grew and improved, few people knew about my struggle. Few people knew how hard those months were for me as an educator. I got better, but only through perseverance and the guidance of great mentors.

We often don't talk about our struggles. We talk instead about our successes. We share our glory with the world and present the greatest of faces. Often that intimidates the world into thinking our struggles don't exist. In fact, those personal moments, those struggles, are what have made us the educators we are today. Embrace your struggle. Take that personal moment and chose to be great while acknowledging that in every person's greatness there will undoubtedly be significant difficulty. No matter how shiny and perfect we all seem, don't be afraid of the imperfect moments. We all struggle. We all fall down. What makes us great as educators is not perfection, but that we continue in spite of our failures to improve for the people around us.

About Brian Costello

Brian Costello is a Digital Innovation Specialist in southern New Jersey. He has previously taught K-2. Brian is the author of *Will McGill & the Magic Hat*, a Google Certified Innovator and Trainer, avid blogger, and education speaker. He is the co-host of the The Suite Talk Show on YouTube, the Director of The Global Audience Project, and owner of BTC2Learn LLC.

The Wind

By Nick Clayton

You know when you are outside and the wind is really blowing; I mean really gusting to where you feel like you may see a house or a wicked witch fly by at any moment? Where your hair slaps you in the face, your hat flies so far you get that moment of "goodbye" with it taunting you before it fades into the distance, your eyes feel like sandpaper and those big gusts make you feel like a kid, dreaming of when you could fly, a moment of liftoff in every big push?

You know when the wind blows in your ears and you feel like you hear every other word of conversation because all you hear is that sound, that sound…like the hollow sound you get when you blow on the top of a bottle to make a ship foghorn, but it doesn't quite work…combined with the rumble of bombs exploding in some country that you heard about on the news all school year where the pictures of students that you wish you could harbor safely in your classroom flash all over the brightly lit pages of digital visual disaster.

That ominous sound has been blowing in and out of my school year, fighting to be noticed, straining to knock it down, to collapse the branches and topple us down in a wiry, sparking mess. That wind is the inevitable. That wind is the fear of the mother, the freezing icy grip over your whole body when something happens to your child and you have no control over it, you just have to leave it up to the unknown, the wait,

the future that is fate,

the fight of your baby,

and the hardest of all to keep up,

the loose hat in that same wind...HOPE.

My year (which I might describe as a year of 180, because we are all trying to turn around to get to a new side of understanding) began like all others, setting up rules and feeding my kids, not knowing if some of them have enough at home to eat a "dinner" as I know dinner to be in my own understanding of it. Maybe they do and it looks different than what I expect for my own life and family; it's not for me to understand or judge... just give, care and HOPE.

Drink coffee and carry on.

My year began with a gale. A gust that toppled me over and stole the wind from my lungs; stealing my teacher voice.

It was a blustery day in September and my hat of hope was held tightly to my head. A student that I had been working to reach, behavior-wise, for over two years was finally starting to mature and respond to my teaching.

To blossom in fact.

He lives in a rough neighborhood (as do most of my brilliant young minds), parents were always difficult to reach when I called about his welfare a couple of times. The day started great with him coming in and working on his morning work, when he suddenly walked to one of my fabulous paraeducators and asked to talk to her in private. He told her he was leaving today to go live with his aunt. He couldn't explain and we took it with a grain of salt because he had been known for telling stories.

He sat down and I had to leave after a sub came to go to an IEP meeting at another school.

On my way back to work I pass by the student's "house" and I see police cars there and an animal control truck. I thought that they had been called to remove animals from the premises

Then the wind began to blow, removing my senses and freezing me to the bone.

I found out when I returned that CPS was at my campus and they were going to take my student to social services. I panicked because I believed he would be a flight risk. He was fine when my assistant principal walked him down and explained what was happening… then the tears came.

Tears from a young man who you would never expect to show any kind of emotion.

He and his brother were removed in the same car together, which is when the school resource officer explained the situation to me.

My hat blew away and it took a while to find again.

This small, young life had been living in a house of horrors; a drug den with five adults on drugs, 20 kids and 18 dogs (two dead) all living in a one bedroom apartment infested with mold, lined with trash. This scene permanently scarred on my brain as one of the biggest gusts ever to hit me.

I went into protective parent mode, ran to the store, bought him and the other kids $400 worth of living supplies and went to be with them at social services.

It was like nothing I have ever experienced.

I was lucky enough to get my student and his brother back to my school the next day… my hat was found, the very next day! Now the student's behavior became out of control, but at least he was back to me and I could try to continue the work I had been doing with him. The wind had calmed.

Then came a dust storm. My student that I had been working with for 2 years at home with health problems lost his guardian, his grandfather who was like family to me and our district, to a heart attack.

The wind died down a little, but then turned into a hurricane that broke down my classroom.

Walking home one day in February, my class jokester, bright, bubbly, "Mr. Personality" of my classroom, was hit by a car and almost killed.

Forget the hat, I am clearing away debris.

He was a broken young man. He was saved from death, but there was major damage to his body and swelling in his brain, stopping him from returning to school.

My classroom was devastated; students still being blown around by the gusts from the aftershocks of storms to follow.

I spent nights blowing the rain away from my windshield, coming in sideways at me, affecting my family.

At school, we are finally beginning to create a shelter from future storms.

However the holes remain.

Unpatched.

The wind still blowing in.

Luckily my students help me keep my hat on.

Because the wind never seems to blow their hats away. They seem to have ways of keeping them on, no matter how little they have, or how rough their neighborhood is, or how much and how hard the wind blows in gusts to try to make them blow away. To try to make them chase hope.

My students are part of my family.

My family is my hat.

They keep the wind from blowing me over.

They are all of the cups of coffee.

They are what keep me walking against the wind, when it blows too hard on the playground, when it threatens to spin my world away, out of control, into chaos.

About Nick Clayton

Nick is a husband and a father of two. He "works" as a 4-6th grade special education teacher in a bright, blustery, Southern California desert. He teaches students using the language of technology and tries, at every chance, to give them opportunities to learn about the world and what is out there for them.

Poetry Selections

Sarah Windisch

Why I Teach
When you say that teaching is a calling
I think you misunderstand
It's not an urge
A desire
I haven't been summoned to teach
No one called me to this
It's who I am
Always was
Even when I was
Convinced I was
Someone else

Best Day Ever
Every time the lightbulb appears over
A student's head
Is the best day
Of teaching

Paper Jam
It never fails that
On the day you forget your coffee
(Or didn't make enough)
There is a line at the (broken) copier
And inside recess
And a message from THAT parent (again)

185

But you never seem to drown.
You break the surface
And see the students
And remember then
That teaching (TEACHING) has nothing
To do with
The copier.

Back in my Day
I was the student
That every teacher loved
Except that one
Who was intimidated by my
Formidable intellect and
Robust vocabulary,
But most of all
Was completely rocked back on her heels
By the fact that
I was comfortable
In my own skin
At the age
Of eleven

Making an Impact
I've heard teaching compared to
Ripples
Fire
Buckets
Candles
Wind

And a million other metaphors
About how what we do
Makes a bigger impact
Than we could ever guess
But if we're completely
Honest with ourselves
We know EXACTLY
How we affect our students
And that's WHY
We are
Teachers.

Go to the Principal's Office
I can't imagine
The patience
Required for being an administrator
Between
Students
Parents
Paperwork
And (let's be honest)
Teachers like me
I'm glad
That it's your job and you love it.
(Mostly)
(I hope)

Standing Firm
Red jacket
Red sign

Red ribbons and
"Wear Red for Ed"
It all matches
The red stroller
I'm pushing in the rain
At this rally
So that you
(My son)
Will not only
Have a great education
But so you
KNOW
How to stand up
For what
You believe in.

First Day of School!
To me,
The first day of school is a smell
It's pencils
And crayons
Soap
And sunshine
Fresh paper
And toothpaste
Under all of that
There is the smell
Of hunger
And thirst
For knowledge

And structure
Food
And love
Acceptance
And grace

Outside the Box
The thing about "Best Practices"
Is that no one
Knows what's
BEST
For your classroom
Students
And style
But YOU
And you've been PRACTICING
Innovating
Iterating
Creating
Since the
Very
First
Day

Working Relationships
If we weren't able
To joke together
About all the terrible things
That happened this
Week,

When I told you
Something sincerely
(Not sarcastically.)
It wouldn't be
So
Sweet.
Thank you.

About Sarah Windisch

Sarah Windisch is
Midcareer music teacher
Idaho native
Her students learn more
Than music inside her classroom
They discover JOY.
(She doesn't always
write haiku but in this case
It was too much fun.)

Why Would Anyone Choose to Teach Seventh Grade?

Joy Kirr

"Why do you teach 7th grade?" is the question most often asked when I tell people what I do. Why would anyone choose middle school??

Why DO I teach 7th grade? The position that I currently have landed in my lap. Every day I am grateful for the choices I made that led me here. However, when I started, I, too, was a bit skeptical. Why DID I want to teach in a middle school?

Over the years, the answer has become clear - these children are still children, and yet they get some (most?) of my humor. I don't understand some of theirs, and maybe that is why I chuckle or outright guffaw at some of the events that occur during the day. I'm writing today to share some of the examples of daily life at my middle school...

We have paper stars hanging from yarn - to share our wishes for ourselves or the world. Seventh graders (like Toby) are still young enough to walk around the room, trying to reach the stars with their heads - to "run into" them" accidentally.

Sometimes you have bad days, too. You try to not let them show. At this age, however, kids catch on. They may ask you if you want to see them dance to make you feel better!

When a student complains about how another teacher doesn't want him talking with his friend, you get to hear emphatic statements such as, "She won't even let us blow our noses together!"

During PARCC (state) testing at our school, we've had a student bleed on the test. We've had a student vomit on the computer. However... the best story I heard during PARCC testing was when Joe got his Chromebook case STUCK on his head... He was simply bored prior to the test starting, put it on (zipper-side down) over his head, and could not get it off! Every time I bring it up, he still gets red.

Riley pointed at me, and while my arm was raised, he put his finger in my armpit! I grabbed it and held on. As I was clutching it, his finger started turning purple. I let go, he apologized, and the next day I wrote a poem about it - to hang on our "poet tree" of course. He and the class loved it. He even came back the next April to ask me to share it with my new classes.

Some of my students are a full head shorter than me. Some of my students are a full head taller than me. Almost all have (or will get) braces during seventh grade. I can't help but empathize. I've been there, and I can relate.

My students become my kids. I know they have parents at home, but I feel so protective of them when they're in my care. This happens to many teachers who see teaching as a lifelong profession, and not just a "job." During three days and two nights at our outdoor education trip, you get to see a new side of your children, and they get to see a new side of you. It's so refreshing to hear, "Are you okay, Mrs. Kirr?" from a student you believe "hates" you during a typical school day.

You meet a child out at bus duty who says she likes the sign in your door that reads, "Not all of us will be sitting in chairs... We are learning how to collaborate and communicate with each other..." because, as she explains, "It shows you care."

When I tell my students I'm going to be absent, and they pout or complain, it's the only complaining I actually don't mind. All others cost $5.00. ;)

When the bell rings to conclude class, I shout, "Have a marvelous Monday" (or some other farewell). Many times, if no one responds, I answer myself in a higher pitch, "You, too, Mrs. Kirr!" I love it when they think it's funny and then some finally DO respond. They still need models of appropriate social interactions.

When it feels like every day is Groundhog Day, it probably is. I know I've been there before. It gives me a sense of calm, knowing that the children in front of me may change, but many of the situations won't.

Seventh graders will tell you when you need a haircut, or when you have a pimple (I thought I was done with puberty 30 years ago!), or when your makeup looks different, or when you're wearing glasses, or if the room smells funny, or if you look tired... They notice EVERYthing. They also pick up on it when you're suffering, and they'll ask if they can help in any way.

As the teacher, when you say words (even if you're just reading them from a text!) such as "fart" or "sex" or "do do," you get silly giggling from around the room, and you reveal a smirk because you just can't hide it.

Seventh graders appreciate transparency. They respect you if you respect them. One student can push another teacher's buttons all day every day, but will be fine as pie in your class if you get to know him and talk to him like a person. Say hello and ask how he is before you slide in that request for any missing work.

Seventh graders are at their most vulnerable. They need a caring heart, a helping hand, and a shoulder when times get tough. When you can connect with a 12 or 13-year-old and she smiles at you, she gets lodged in your heart forever.

Why do I teach 7th grade? They keep me young. They reinvigorate me, even as they give me new gray hairs. Sometimes we cry together, but most often we laugh together - every day. And then some of us (Who, me??) cry once again on the last day of the school year as we sign yearbooks... I love this adventure we're on together, and my wish is that they do, too!

About Joy Kirr

Joy currently teaches 7th grade English Language Arts at Thomas Middle School in Arlington Heights, IL. She was first a special education teacher working with deaf & hard-of-hearing students, and next became a reading specialist and National Board Certified. She is passionate about students owning their own learning. One of her blogs resides at http://geniushour.blogspot.com/, and her book called *Shift This: How to Implement Gradual Change for Massive Impact in Your Classroom* was released in May, 2017.

Confessions of an Ordinary Teacher

Eric Hayes

Benjamin Franklin once said, "The doorstep to the temple of wisdom is a knowledge of our own ignorance." I found this to be certainly true in my case because the longer I teach, the more I realize how little I know and how much I still have to learn. Whereas, some would consider this an odd confession from a teacher, it has become my badge of honor. I find myself freely sharing my failures with my students and no longer attempting to hide any perceived shortcomings. However, I was not always this way.

I entered the teaching profession with a burning desire to share my love of learning and help my community. With a head full of knowledge, I entered my first assignment in a middle school in a poor neighborhood absolutely convinced that I could inspire my students. After all, I knew that once they saw how passionate I was, they would pay rapt attention in class, but how wrong I was. Within a week, I had come crashing down to reality as I discovered that my students, who were reading significantly below grade level, had no interested in what I was selling. They told me that the streets offered them a better education, and they saw little point to school. I wish I could say that I immediately reassessed my situation and took steps to create a learning environment well-suited for them, but that is not what I did.

Something many of us are very good at is explaining away what we do not agree with or simply downplaying what does not fit in our world view. Being quite good at this, I reasoned that there was nothing wrong with my teaching and the problem had to be my students. I successfully managed to convince myself that my students did not appreciate the wonderful education they were receiving. I continued with this false belief, sadly, for far too long, and I would probably still feel this way had it not been for a drastic change in circumstances.

My wife and I moved to another state seeking new opportunities and a change of scenery. What I could not have imagined is how this move would forever change me as a teacher. Having taken a teaching job mid-year, I soon learned that my position was a temporary one, and I would have to look for another job. Thankfully, I found one in a neighboring county as an Inclusion Math teacher in a high school, which is funny because math had always been my weakest subject. Not only did I find myself having to relearn algebra, but I also had to to learn what it meant to be a co-teacher. To make matters worse, the school year had already started, and I was going to begin in late October. If you have never worked as a co-teacher, then try imagining going from having your own classroom to working in someone else's. If that does not sound daunting enough, imagine if you are assigned to teach a subject that you disliked as child and with a teacher who has a completely different educational philosophy than you. If you really like a challenge, try doing all of this after the school year had begun. That is how I started my experience as an inclusion teacher.

Being in a new teaching assignment and in working in an unfamiliar subject area, I discovered myself as a teacher. I finally was given the chance to see things from my students' standpoint. Imagine having to grapple with trying to stay one step ahead of your class and being so lost, at times, that you have to ask a student to help you figure out how to solve a certain problem.

These early years in inclusion seem like a lifetime ago, but I will never forget the feeling of being useless. However, something strange happened. Having been thrusted into the role of being a learner again, the students viewed me as someone that they could trust, or maybe they just felt bad for me because I seemed so lost. Although I had not asked for it, students started opening up to me and asking me what I thought of their teacher or if I really liked math. Let me tell you one thing I quickly discovered-they were less than enthused about their learning. I repeatedly heard students ask the teacher of record, "When are we ever going to use this [what they were learning] in life?" a question I had heard many times in my own class. Her response was the same as mine had been, 'You are going to need to know this for some sort of standardized test.' However, this time I was not the one uttering these hollow words; it was someone else, yet I was the one hearing what essentially was rubbish. This teacher, despite being quite skilled at offering wonderful mathematical explanations, had not stopped to reflect on the why-Why did her students really need to learn this material? Of course, these students were unmotivated.

It saddens me to think that it took three years of teaching for me to finally figure out what my students need. I have spent the rest of my career reminding myself that students do not need a person full of knowledge who does not care about them nor do they need us, their teachers, to tell them that what we are teaching is valuable if they are unable to see it. Armed with this new understanding, I could not help but feel a profound sadness for my previous students I taught those first three years. To these students, I want to say one thing, you deserved better. I am sorry that I did not take the time to get to know you as individuals. I deeply regret force feeding you content that was completely irrelevant to your lives and being angry when you were not thankful. I thought you were the problem, but all along I was the problem

Now you know one of my deepest secrets. Why am I sharing it with you? I am afraid that if I do not keep reminding myself of this revelation I will fall back into my old thinking. I force myself to stop and reflect on what I am doing as a teacher. I am not the bearer of content, but the molder of people. I do not teach to get students to pass a test, I teach to them to think critically. When I find that my content seems to have to be irrelevant, than I seek to give it meaning. When I feel limited by the people I work with, I look beyond my school walls to a larger global network of other teachers trying to make a difference. The truth is that all of us are in the same boat. We often do not appreciate our true power because we are trapped by archaic systems and rigid programs that seek to limit us and our students. All of this can be frustrating, but we are not without hope because we have the power to think for ourselves and examine what our students really need from us. What is it that they need? They need us to believe in them, to empathize with them, and to innovate our practices for them. Sounds pretty daunting, does it not? As the book *Kids Deserve It* says, "We must be in the business of removing boundaries for kids."

About Eric Hayes

Eric Hayes is an international educator with over 11 years of teaching experience who is on a simple mission-do right by kids and keep growing professionally. He is currently living in Brazil with his wife and two cats.

Making an Impact

It is our choices, Harry, that show what we truly are, far more than our abilities.

- Dumbledore

A Breath of Fresh Air

Aubrey Yeh

At the beginning of my junior year of high school, my mom was diagnosed with cancer, and she went through chemotherapy for most of that year. Being the oldest of three kids in the house, I put a lot of pressure on myself to help care for my younger siblings while my mom was not feeling well. At the same time, I was dealing with the fact that I wasn't quite ready to be grown up yet!

It was hard. It took me a long time to tell my friends what was going on - not because I didn't want them to know, but just because I didn't know how to tell them. How did something that heavy fit into regular high school chatter?

"What are you wearing to homecoming?"

"Oh my gosh, that assignment took me two hours!"

"Hey guys, my mom has cancer."

Yeah, I couldn't see that going very well, so I kept quiet instead.

I became a master masker and went through the day as normally as I could. I kept handing in all of my assignments, participating in class, and getting good grades. What else could I do? The routine was comfortable and familiar, and I knew where I fit in. It's what everyone expected of me, and it seemed easiest to just go with those expectations. But, over time, it definitely took its toll on me. The stress built up and the pressure grew.

My saving grace through this year was a teacher at the school, "Profe". I actually had never had him as a teacher, but he was a youth pastor at my church, so we knew each other fairly

200

well. He also knew what was going on in my life. I began a habit of stopping by his room every day at lunch. It was only a few minutes, maybe five, but in these minutes I could be REAL. He would ask me how I was doing that day, and if I replied, "Not so good," it wouldn't be a big deal. I could share if my mom had just had a treatment or that our house was filling up with hats or that I had a hard time listening to my friends complain about getting a B on the last math test - didn't they know there were more important things in life? No matter where I was at emotionally on that day, his reaction wasn't surprise or pity (which I dreaded), just empathy and listening.

I started to live for these daily check-ins. If I was having a rough morning, my refrain would be, "Only a few more classes, and then I can go talk to Profe." It was like getting the chance to breathe after putting a show on underwater for the rest of the day. With my home life feeling uncertain and the rest of my life feeling like a bad imitation, his room was my safe haven.

As an educator now, I know how valuable those five minutes which Profe shared with me at lunchtime can be. They equal grading a few assignments, responding to a few emails, or even a quick run to the bathroom! Never once did Profe complain, and never once did I feel like a burden. I'm sure it cost him something - he probably stayed later, came earlier, or took more work home in order to give me those few minutes per day. But he was willing to do that for his students - he was willing to do that for ME.

What strikes me as profound is how simple this gesture was. Really, all that happened is that he said hi, asked me how I was doing, and listened to the answer. Isn't that something we could do for students all of the time? Yet how often do I get caught up in my busy work and fail to truly listen to the person who is in front of me? How many of my students are stuck in their own underwater shows, desperately searching for a breath? Will I take the time to give them that breath of fresh air?

Through my junior year, Profe was my lifeline connecting my home life with my school life. As my mom finished her treatment and went into remission, my lunchtime visits became less and less frequent, but they left a powerful imprint on my life. As I went into my senior year, I could not go back to being the carefree student of my youth, but the load did begin to lighten. I had finally made it back to dry land, a little wiser and more mature than before. Even as I embarked on new journeys, I never forgot the safety of being real, known, and cared for by a teacher. And now, I find myself in that same position of being a teacher. There are students right in front of me with all kinds of things going on in their lives. In the midst of my busy days, I never want to forget that asking a question or listening to my students talk might be a lifeline for them. We, as educators, are in a people business - let us never forget to take the time to care for the person beneath each student in our class!

About Aubrey Yeh

Aubrey Yeh is currently a 5th-8th grade music teacher in Broomfield, Colorado who will take tea or hot chocolate over coffee any day! Throughout her career, she has taught music, science, and literacy to 1st-12th grade students, and she is currently pursuing a degree in educational leadership as well. Aubrey thrives on continuing to find ways to support all students, no matter what is going on in their lives. You can connect with her on Twitter at @ms_a_yeh or follow her adventures through her blog: blog.msayeh.com.

Red Clowns: A Male Educator's Perspective

Sean Eichenser

In *The House on Mango Street*, Sandra Cisneros tells the story of Esperanza Cordero, a 12 year old Chicana girl growing up in a Latino neighborhood of Chicago, through a series of short, prose poetry-style vignettes. She talks about growing up, noticing boys, going to school, and walking that tightrope between being a girl and becoming a woman. Many teachers over the years have taught *The House on Mango Street*, and with good reason; it's a phenomenal book and reaches my teenage students in portions of their lives that no adult could understand. My girls see themselves reflected in Esperanza's story, even decades after it was originally written. My boys see the world from a perspective that they'd never considered. I love teaching this book, but every year I spend about three days in nervous trepidation.

Any teacher who has taught *The House on Mango Street* knows which vignette causes this mild panic. "Red Clowns." Near the end of the collection of stories, Esperanza is deserted by her friend at a carnival, and is sexually assaulted by a group of boys. The story implies that Esperanza is raped by these boys, while her disjointed account only describes the look of the clown decorations. I worry about this story, and reading it with the kids.

In the era of memes and "Meninists" my 8th grade students use the language of the oppressed, disadvantaged, and neurodivergent as a joke. Once, when I called a student "dude" before asking him to take a seat, he responded "did you just assume my gender, Mr. Eichenser?" And my class laughed, big-grinned laughs. In their reality they don't know any "out" transgender individuals, so the hurtful or "non-PC" images and memes they see on the internet normalize the casual hatred of those individuals. In the quest for internet notoriety, strangers will step on anyone's neck for a retweet. As adults, we recognize the pettiness and cruelty in these jokes; but for my students it shapes their worldview. I have little patience for the "it's just a joke" crowd.

But that's not why I lose sleep for three days, especially this year. In this 8th grade class of about 110, there are 8 young girls, my students, who have been sexually abused or otherwise assaulted. This is, unfortunately, not an anomaly. According to RAINN, "one in nine girls and one in fifty-three boys under the age of eighteen experience sexual abuse or assault at the hands of an adult." Essentially, this means I have a student or two in each class period of the day who has experienced an assault directly. I have sat in meetings that run the spectrum: parents who console their kids, parents who blame their kids, parents who invalidate their kids. I worry about how my students will cope; I worry about what other students will say to those victims.

I plan on reading the story aloud together on Monday. The Friday before, I tell the kids that, next week, we will be reading a story that involves some heavy themes like assault, and if that's too uncomfortable to please contact me or email me. A bespectacled boy in the back yells "#triggered" in a way that I hear the hashtag. Again, the jokes. In each class, I wait to see if those girls will make eye contact with me. None do. My stomach continues to churn. I have images in my head of girls reliving their experiences in my class, or being harangued by insensitive boys. Come Monday, I receive no emails.

I read the story all the way through rather than pass it off onto another student. It's short, but descriptive. My girls look around at one another, and my boys squirm awkwardly in their seats. A part of me likes how uncomfortable the boys look; that they are confronting a reality that's different from their own.

When I finish reading, one of my boys comments "wait, how old is Esperanza right now?"

I bump the question to the class, to which someone responds "about 12 or 13."

The boy's face stretches in horror. "That's messed up, she's not even 18!"

One of my girls, a girl I'm worried about, whips around and the air buzzes like that moment just before a lightning strike. "There's no right age for rape. It's not better or worse that she's a kid." She asserts this as the universal truth that it is. The boy, usually argumentative, agrees quickly.

"Her friend [Sally] shouldn't have left her!" another boy says, attempting sympathy, "Esperanza should be mad at her!" The comment hangs heavy in silence.

"It's no one's fault but her attacker's." I reply, "The first thing we say when someone is assaulted is 'what was she wearing?' or 'why was she out with him?' That's not acceptable. She has every right to be mad and upset and there's only one person to blame; it's not her fault." The class is quiet and it feels like one of those rare moments where they're actually listening instead of just looking at me. Teachers know how different the air feels in those moments.

I ask each girl I've been worried about to hang back after class, citing an after-school activity or homework help. One-on-one, I stay seated at my desk, but tell each of them how proud I am, how well they handled today, and that they did a great job. In turn, they each beam a big smile; a few tear up. For many, the fear of having their pain mocked was more than they could bear. Some expressed gratitude at the ability to talk about it, some simply nodded. The knot in my stomach began to untie itself with each passing class period.

The last girl, arguably whose wounds were still the freshest and who had been having the toughest time in school, said something different. "You're the first boy-" then she stopped to correct herself, "first man to say it's not my fault."

I was stunned. When I began to reply she interrupted me. "I know you don't like hugs, Mr. Eichenser, so…thanks." She turned heel and walked out of my classroom, grinning from ear to ear. I sat at my desk, trying to wrap my brain around the fact that I, somehow, was the first male in her life to say that her rape was not her fault.

I'm sure there is research that says I shouldn't have said what I did, or that sharing my values so explicitly could land me in professional trouble. It's worth noting that I teach in the relatively liberal city in a fairly progressive district. I feel as if I'm on the right side of history. I cannot say it's not my place to speak on these things, because otherwise there is a misogynistic media and a sphere of social websites to influence them. For many of my kids, I'm the only male teacher they see all day in their elementary school experience. This is not to say my words carry more weight or more importance than any of my colleagues; but it is to say that I'm in the position of being a role model for my students. In a weird way, from my students' perspective, my female co-workers speak for themselves; I speak for all men-kind.

Now, this here's for the fellas. Gentlemen, I implore you: talk about this stuff in your classroom. Be the example. Model respect for your boys and girls, even in the "off-times." As backwards as this sentiment may sound out of context: sometimes they just need to hear a man say these things. That assault is never okay, that porn isn't realistic, that girls are not objects to be collected or conquered. I can't speak for my boys and girls who are searching for where they belong in the LGBT community. I realize this essay can come off pretty heteronormative. I'm sure there are voices out in the world who can speak to that; and I don't want to take up that space. But we need to not be afraid of discussing these issues.

For all teachers, regardless of genders, we need to bring literature into our classrooms that discuss these issues. We cannot let our stomachs churn and shy away from what makes us uncomfortable, because we cannot wait for the memes to raise our students. I will continue to read *The House on Mango Street* every year with my 8th graders and give my students the space to feel safe. I will continue to incorporate this text with these themes in the hope that one day, it won't be necessary.

About Sean Eichenser

Sean Eichenser is an 8th grade Language Arts teacher in Chicago, IL. At the time of this writing, he's been teaching for three years and has loved every day. He lives in Chicago with his girlfriend, whom he met at Illinois State University, and his dog, who he met at a rescue shelter.

I Love You Enough

Stephanie Dingle

To My Precious Students,

By now, I hope I've told you more than a lot of times that I love you. I know that sometimes my words are directed at the class as a whole, and sometimes I say things like, "Look, I love y'all, and I'd take a bullet for any one of you, but right now you're driving me crazy..." Other times you've heard, "I just love y'all so much. I've never had such an awesome class." But the message is the same, and I do love you. And I'd like to think that, in the event of something crazy and/or catastrophic, that I'd actually shove you out of the way and jump in front of a bullet for you. (Please let's not find out, though...)

The point is that I love you. Period. Plain and simple. For a moment, though, I'd like to add a word to that statement: enough. I love you enough.

Know the word is not intended to serve as a limitation. Instead, think of it as a means of expansion, of clarification, of depth.

I love you enough to sit with you when you're struggling, to ask questions and help you flesh out what's bothering you, to hand you the bathroom pass and a tissue so you can wipe the snot from your nose and mascara from your eyes.

I love you enough to see the bruise underneath the four layers of concealer you're wearing and to give the whole class a free-write journal prompt just so you can have a place to write all the words you can't bring yourself to say out loud. I love you enough to slip you a Post-it note that lets you know you can come talk to me if you need a shoulder. I love you enough to wrap my arms around you so you can understand that love doesn't have to hurt.

I love you enough to call you out and then call your mom. To hold you accountable. To walk you to the office when you show up to my room smelling like weed and poor choices. To place my arm lovingly around your shoulder and remind you that the mistakes (and the good choices) you make now will impact you for weeks, months, years to come.

I love you enough to give you the failing grade you earned. I love you so much that I will listen to you beg, tears running down your face, for a passing grade because you so desperately want to stay on the sports team, keep your cell phone, or attend that party your parents said you could only attend if you're passing, and then explain to you why I will not bump your grade to passing. I love you so much that I will risk your frustration - your anger, even - so that you will learn how to earn rather than how to beg, how to work rather than how to expect.

I love you enough to see you in the hallway with a boy that has nothing but wrong intentions and turn you in a direction that moves you away from him. To tell you that you're beautiful and smart and worth more than what he sees in you. To walk you to your class and knock on the door and deliver you to the arms of another teacher that only wants you to put your potential to work.

I love you enough to pull you in the hallway and tell you you're acting like a jerk, a fake mean-girl, a rumor mill. To remind you that you don't have to hurt other people in order to get attention, that you can be kind and nice and treat other people the way you'd like them to treat you. To remind you to love yourself as you are instead of pretending to be something you're not. That you're worth that kind of love.

I love you enough to stop my lesson right smack in the middle because I see your face is full of something that does not resemble school or literature or writing and to give you a few minutes to just vent. I love you enough to ask you what's going on, to give you a safe space to speak or write out what's on your mind, and then to spend some time reading your words and speaking silent prayers over you while you're in my room but you'd maybe rather be anywhere else.

I love you enough to know that your parents are struggling or that your dad left or that your mom is overcome with addiction or that your brother has been arrested or that you're not sure where you will live next month because nobody can make rent.

I love you enough to know that the condom that fell out of your pocket represents an insecurity that runs so deep you don't even begin to know how to address it, who to turn to, what to say. And I love you enough to ask you about it, even when it's unbearably uncomfortable and you can't even make eye contact with me because you aren't sure how, at 14, you might actually have to tell your mom your girlfriend is pregnant.

I love you enough to listen as you cuss me out and yell at me before hurling a desk against the wall and slamming the door as you leave. I love you enough to sit in the hall with you while you calm down so you can know that I see that, at the core of your meltdown, your heart is breaking and you just don't know how to piece it back together. I see your hurt rather than your outburst. I see you.

I see you, and I love you.

As the summer approaches and we prepare to part ways, please know that you have been the joy of my year, even in moments of difficulty when we've all just wanted to turn around and run for the hills. You are my most precious students, and I love you dearly.

I love you enough.

Please don't ever forget it.

Love,

Mrs. Dingle

About Stephanie Dingle

Stephanie Dingle is a teacher in Garland ISD and currently teaches English I and AP Literature at Rowlett High School. She enjoys running, reading, and spending time with family, especially her two little boys. Stephanie has taught for thirteen years and hopes to continue for many years to come.

No Coffee - Just Add Love

Michele Osinski

When Mari, my sweet digi-daughter, asked me to write for her project, I said "YES!" I love to write and take far too little time in my days to put "pen to paper". Though outside of my doodling, I don't much use pen and paper anymore. I love using a computer to compose, and being able to cut and paste to move ideas and sentences around. I also love the ability to let some writing "simmer" (a term I stole from a children's author years ago) and go back to it later. Those of us who are very particular about our sentence construction and vocabulary appreciate the revision opportunities that word processing affords us. For those of us who "did" college without computers and/or the internet, writing is SO much easier. No matter the task at school, I'll be the first to ask, "Is there a digital version of this?" or "Want me to make a Form for that?" I am all about finding the most efficient way!

I suppose that there is a most efficient way that Mari makes her coffee (aka stopping by Starbucks). Or it may differ by the coffee drinker. I don't know. I own a coffee maker, but it rarely gets put into use other than when my REAL daughter is in town from Nashville for a visit. Even then, I have to get a refresher course on what kind of coffee I'm supposed to buy and she has to brew it all herself. I've never developed a coffee habit. I never could put enough cream or sugar in it to mask the bitter aftertaste. I REALLY tried when my ex-husband was studying for the Bar Exam and developed a coffee habit. Nope. Still nope.

I do have a different habit. A LOVE habit. Even though it has been more than 20 years since I have had a personal/romantic relationship sapping my love carafe, I have used this time to rediscover the many different nuances of love, and how I want to continue to love others.

My first step in passing the love cup has been to continue my mindset of RELATIONSHIPS. It starts in my classroom, but extends to friendships old and new, family, and strangers. If all of us were to treat others as if we had a relationship with each and every one of them, the world would be a better place! In my classroom, my goal during the first days is to get to know at least one interest or passion of each student, and not through a "Getting to Know You" worksheet: through one-one-one, face-to-face conversation. Our first days together are focused on all of the fun things we'll get to do rather than the "Thou Shalt Not" rules. That's not to say that we don't have expectations for behavior, but those just boil down to personal responsibility and BE NICE! There isn't a situation we can face in our classrooms that cannot be handled with grace and conversation. Mutual respect. I would never expect my students to respect me if I have not acted respectfully to them. As the late, WONDERFUL Rita Pierson said (among other things!), "Kids don't learn from people they don't like." And George Washington Carver added, "All learning is understanding relationships."

Throughout the years, I have made every opportunity to get my students' competition schedules (soccer, basketball, football, taekwondo) away from school, and then I try to make it there to support my student - at least once. This started back in my 3rd and 4th years of teaching (1987/1988). I had developed a relationship with my student Duane and his younger brother,

Derrick, who were both in my class. I was teaching a 4/5/6 grade (yes… THREE grade levels!) "GATE" class which required a LOT of tap dancing… good thing I was young! I was able to attend a couple of Duane's and Derrick's taekwondo competitions and several of Jamal, Vince, JD, and Sammy's football games. My girls were not involved in sports, but I think that just by attending the boys' games, they knew that I sincerely cared about them too.

Last summer, I found out that many of these students from Johnson Elementary had found me on Facebook. One by one, they started sending "friend" requests, and I started to giggle. I recognized the many names although they had all grown up and changed so much! I am sure my grey hair surprised them as well. I found out that they were looking for me so that they could invite me to a big party that they were having. Many of them had remained in each other's lives and were hosting a 40th birthday party for their squad. 40. Oh Wow.

I did attend the party.

TEARS. Tears of joy and laughter. Someone's arms were constantly around me. I just kept hearing "REMEMBER WHEN…" and then they'd all break down, laughing hysterically. But there were also some more quiet "remember when's" when talking about our life inside our classroom: B-3; I still remember the number. Several of these ADULTS shared that they were always happy to go to school; wondering what would be offered that day. They remembered specific art lessons and me having the patience to teach them calligraphy. They remembered getting to sing a Michael Jackson song (Man in the Mirror) for "graduation" instead of some tired old song that everyone else had always sung. They talked about getting to hold MOON ROCKS. They talked about feeling safe - in a neighborhood that was often the victim of gun violence. We all remembered Tony's funeral. He'd been hit by a car on Christmas day, riding his new bike.

I confessed how Mrs. Martins and Mrs. Clarkson had made me feel worthless when they pulled together a unit on Martin Luther King, Jr. for our grade levels. I had admitted that due to my age (24 at the time) and upbringing (Newport Beach, California), I wasn't exposed to Dr. King and his accomplishments. However, I was excited to learn alongside my students. I had not met or talked to a person of color until I was an adult, a freshman at Cal State Fullerton. It wasn't my fault. I didn't know any better. But I wanted to know and learn. The other teachers decided to create a rotation of activities for the students, and I ... well, they guessed I could show a movie (then I wouldn't have a chance to say something stupid). This hurt me badly. I have always been honest with my students about my strengths and shortcomings.

My former students surrounded me with hugs and love, letting me know that not once did they feel "lesser than" in my eyes, and never felt pre-judged. They knew I saw them as wonderful individuals who had just as much to teach me as I them. They admitted that although they were surprised by Mrs. Johnson's behavior, they expected as much from Mrs. Martins. "She was a mean old cow with a huge chip on her shoulder." RELATIONSHIPS, I told them. We had relationships, and we obviously still loved each other. Mrs. Martins hadn't create relationships with her students and she was remembered as "a mean old cow".

Knowing that this piece of writing for Mari's project was going to be about love and relationships, I asked a few of the "kids" most active on Facebook to send me a memory. Here are some of their thoughts 30 years later:

Miss Kelli (center) sent me this photo, on the day of their "graduation" from 6th grade. Angelica (left), Kelli, and Julanda (right) were with me for 4th, 5th, and 6th grades! They're still friends and remembered that I was like an auntie to them. An auntie who didn't tell their moms any secrets. They wanted to say they thought of me like a mom who didn't get mad, but I had to remind them that I was only 25 at the time and they were 11!

Vincent wanted me to share this: "She was my favorite teacher, and one of the only teachers I can still remember to this day. What made her stand out to me was her positive energy. I think teachers, and people overall, underestimate that aspect of teaching. She greeted us every morning at the stairs to our classroom with a smile and genuine caring of how you were feeling. Kids know when somebody wants to be there. Over the rest of my school years, I encountered many teachers that you could tell just wanted to make it through the day."

When we connected early last year, Julanda told me, "I've been looking for you FOREVER!" As far as memories of our time together, she sent this message: "I entered my 4th grade class, and thought we had no teacher. I looked around and figured there was a teacher's aid because the woman that was standing in the front of the class was so young. As she began to welcome us to the GATE class, I then realized that Mrs. Osinski was actually my teacher! My memories of her are so vivid. She was definitely a strong influence in my life. I was in her class for three years: from the 4th-6th grade so she helped me become the woman that I am today. Whenever I am asked who my favorite teacher was, I always say Mrs. Michele Osinski. And that sentiment is shared by my elementary schoolmates. We all adored her, and we still do!"

It has been very important to my longevity and my happiness in my career to model "good human" behavior. I admit my faults; I apologize when I'm wrong. I talk about myself and my life, and my children. My students and I are with each other so much of each day that I want them to feel part of a familial relationship. As I head toward my "twilight years" in the classroom, I must continue to develop those relationships: cups of love. And obviously, my cup runneth over. Perhaps, in another 30 years, I'll have developed a taste and will be having a cup of coffee with some of my students in this year's class.

About Michele Osinski

Michele is proud to be finishing her 32nd year in the classroom, primarily in fifth grade. In the past few years, her love for teaching and learning has been re-invigorated by working with EdTech. She has truly found her "tribe" and hopes that she can contribute some ideas along with some wisdom as she meets new friends and enjoys new experiences.

On a personal level, she finally finished her MA in Humanities (History/Philosophy emphasis) in 2011; taking college courses with a computer and the internet was FUN! She has a daughter, Keegan, who is a full-time librarian at the Divinity Library at Vanderbilt University in Nashville. Her son, Brendan, is a civil engineer with a large-build company based in Irvine, CA. The birdies having successfully flown from the nest, she enjoys her peace and quiet and travel as much as possible.

New Message!

Nick Brierley

Lately, I have become more aware of the many messages that we as teachers send to our students. Of course, we communicate with words. We are ever-increasingly communicating with technology. Endless emails, the introduction of Google Classroom and of course, the feedback loop moves faster than ever. Our actions show much we care, or how indifferent we are. And of course body language tells our students that despite our words and actions, what we are really feeling and thinking. All of this combines to create the message. In 2017 (and many other years for that matter) it is this message that dictates the calibre of educator that we choose to be.

I was brought to a rude awakening recently by an experience that I shared with my two-year-old nephew, Thomas. He only recently turned 2 and despite what others tell me, I believe him to be the most brilliant young boy I have ever met. And it is because of this that I feel it is essential, that the messages that he receives (not only from his uncle 'Ni') are supremely important.

One evening after a long family dinner, I felt a tug on my shirt, then my hand as I finished the usual post-dinner Brierley cup of tea. Thomas says 'Tom the toot! Tom toot!'. For those who don't speak 2, this means it is time for Thomas The Tank Engine. What a fantastic show that has touched generations of young people and families alike! Of course, we can watch Tom the toot! I love Tom the toot.

I am acutely aware of most things that we watch with Thomas on television and Thomas The Tank Engine is one show that we can definitely trust in it's message for young people. Or so I thought. Oh, how wrong I was.

We could have watched the 2017 computer generated, sing-a-long version of Thomas, but I'm a bit of a classicist. With YouTube at the ready, we watched an episode from 1984 called 'The Sad Story of Henry'. Henry was always a fun character, but a wiki I found puts it best by describing him as 'arrogant' and 'vain'. But that's fine, because it's Thomas, right? I can count on Thomas, right?

This episode finds Henry chugging away across the Island of Sodor in what some might call light rain. Henry's vanity kicks into gear quickly and to savour his precious red and green coat, he parks himself in a tunnel, he says, until the rain ceases. The things is, he never comes out. The Fat Controller (as we used to call him, now referred to as Sir Topham Hatt) orders him out and the townsfolk try both pushing and pulling. No luck. Thomas enters the scene to try to push him out too, but again, no luck. At this point, with Henry digging his heels in, I assume this to be some form of anxiety, depression, lack of esteem (ahem..) or even classic narcissism.

If Henry was a student, how would you react? Any teacher with a heart knows exactly what they would do. It's obvious. But what unfolds next is awful.

The Fat Controller says, and I quote, "We'll take away your rails and leave you here for always and always and always." Wait, what? Leave you here for always and always and always. Is that what we do? We just strand, then desert anyone who doesn't do what we say? Forever?

It got worse before it got better. He followed through with it. The next scene has rail workers removing the lines leading out of the tunnel. Then built a wall of bricks with just enough space between the wall and the roof to see the world he would no longer be a part of for always and always and always.

It is at this point that I divert my attention away from the story, and focus on Thomas so keenly watching what is happening. Should I be worried? What kind of message is this episode giving such a young child? Then it clicked. It's a children's television show, with a short running time to boot. All children's shows end up with happy endings. So it'll be all fine, the message will be happily clarified and we can go on with the next episode soon enough.

Nope.

Firstly, two other trains (his friends) race past Henry and taunt him with words and sounds. And it was at that point that Ringo Starr, (former Beatle and Thomas The Tank Engine narrator) shattered any hopes that the message of this episode would recover. And I quote, 'Poor Henry had no steam to answer. His fire had gone out. Soot and dirt from the tunnel had spoiled his lovely green paint and red stripes anyway. He wondered if he would ever be allowed to pull trains again. I think he deserved his punishment, don't you?'

'Don't you?!'

No, I don't. We're talking about a sentient machine who has been bricked up in a tunnel. Forever. So, no. I don't think he deserved his punishment, Ringo.

It was at this stage, that we stopped watching Thomas for the night. And we have not gone back to the gloomy first series from 1984 and have since stuck to the glossy, embossed, chirpy and colourful Thomas and Friends of 2017. Thomas hopped off my lap and I was left to ponder what I had done.

What message was I advocating by showing this? I thought for a long while, and consulted some friends around potential meanings or subtexts in The Sad Story of Henry.

Some potential messages included:

"Kids need to go outside and play rather than to stay inside and worry about the rain." Fair.

"Children should get in line and listen to their betters." Mmmm.

"Stay in line, or the Man will get you. And he will get you bad." In a way, it is true?

"Still plenty of room in the tunnel for bad little boys and girls..." The message is fear?

"Brick by brick, his doom will be sealed." Quite literally. But I don't like how this sounds.

"Trains are boring. They're just long cars." Right.

"THIS IS WHAT YOU GET HENRY. THIS IS WHAT YOU GET WHEN YOU MESS WITH THE FAT CONDUCTOR'S SCHEDULE." Again, kind of true? But not a great message.

It was at this point, that my thoughts became introspective. How aware am I about the messages that I am sending to students. I'm sure that there is a moral, value or something similar in The Sad Story of Henry, but it definitely isn't obvious and it missed the mark. Do I miss the mark? And how often?

I remembered a student that I had in my class some years ago. For the purposes of this article, let's call him Jayden.

Jayden was in my class at a time where I had unintentionally garnished a reputation for myself as the 'behaviour teacher'. With this crown, came the expectation that if there was a grade perceived to be 'difficult', that I would be considered as an option for them as classroom teacher for a year. That's OK and there is nothing wrong with that, but it can be draining. This class presented a challenge as usual and I was confident in helping these young learners learn, be happy, want to come to school and get along with each other. Most students seemed to, for the most part, respond well to my lessons and I. Except Jayden.

His behaviour had managed to progressively pick up speed on the downward slope. In classes like this, I found that the recipe for success was simply an avoidance of negative reinforcement, regular and encouraging positive reinforcement and a key focus on relationship building. It also helps to avoid having the parent or carer be the 'first port of call'. To build those quality, trusting relationships, the vast number of minor (and some major) issues and problems must first and foremost be worked out in class between teacher and student. And it worked on everyone, except Jayden.

We were at a stage where little to no classwork was being completed. Jayden was actively disturbing his friends and classmates so that they couldn't learn. And finally, he was actively interrupting my teaching so I couldn't give the other students what they needed. This may have been a variety of noises, phrases, actions and occasionally violence. I thought my patience was would have stacked up to be pretty resistant but I was becoming more wrong about that. For the first time in my teaching career, I was struggling and didn't have a way out.

To fix this, I had to change the message that Jayden was hearing. We would now be learning in a one way classroom. And that way was my way. I was in charge. I was the adult, he was the child. I was the teacher, he was the student. I stopped listening to excuses and reason. I ignored his outbursts and squeals. I wasn't going to give any more attention to the student that didn't want to learn. I wasn't going to show that I cared about the student that didn't care about my other students. I was the classroom teacher. What I say goes because I was the boss.

It was at this point, that my passion for this job went out the window.

I even applied for other jobs and we were only in September which was three months short of the end of the school year. I dreaded getting up in the morning. And before I knew it, I wasn't going to school anymore, I was going to work.

It was at this point that the penny dropped. I had doubled down on bad behaviour, rudeness and coarse language, and fired back in the most professional way I knew.

My message wasn't coming from a place that I was proud of. I certainly wasn't the teacher I wanted to be. And I was even less proud of the fact that I was not the person that I wanted to be. This situation I had found myself in would have to end. So in a last ditch effort, I decided to get it together.

So one day, I asked Jayden to see him at lunch. We needed to talk. We needed to talk because I wasn't teaching, he wasn't learning and it was at a point where relationships and impact on other students were being severely affected. So after the bell sounded at lunch, we stayed behind just inside the classroom door so that anyone passing by could see and hear our conversation.

Firstly, I asked him how his day was going. He shrugged.

"Why do you think you're here, mate?"

Another shrug. He looks down at his feet swinging below the chair.

"Jayden. I feel like things haven't been going well at the moment. I feel like things haven't been right for a while."

His eyes move upwards from his feet, to make eye contact with mine.

"Jayden, I'm worried about you, mate. I care about you and I care about your learning."

It was then that his eyes welled up with tears. Not crying, but a stoic look of determination to not let the lump in the throat get the better of him.

"If you don't mind, I'm going to call Mum. I feel like she might be able to help us to work out what is happening in our classroom. She cares about you too. And I know she wants you to be happy, just like I do."

"OK," he said.

I spoke with Jayden's mother later that day. What I heard forced me to realise that my message that I had been sending Jayden was completely off.

Jayden's father had recently developed a serious addiction to ice. For a number of reasons, including a overloaded work schedule, deadlines and other mental pressures had driven him to heavy and frequent use of methamphetamines. Linked to this was a series of incidences of domestic violence where not only Jayden's mother was seriously hurt, but the Jayden and his sister frequently felt the force of this man's ice-induced rage.

The messages that I had been sending were ones of authority, dominance and compliance at all costs. The messages that Jayden needed were ones of care, trust, hope and generosity of not just time, but spirit.

Over the next few months, things changed. Because I changed them.

I was in constant contact with Jayden's mother as she worked hard to find a new home, free from the frequent violence and abuse that the family had come to know. Jayden knew that I was speaking to her. Not to check in with her about behaviour, but about his learning. The focus on improving his learning was the core focus of our discussions, and we seemed to be speaking about behaviour less and less as the year drew to a close.

I wanted to know how Jayden felt about the class, his learning, his progress and about me as his teacher. I needed to know what impact the recent changes in our classroom, and in our relationship was having on his little mind. Had I gone too far? Would he realise that I was trying to help him that whole time? Would it be possible to rebuild that trust between us? I waited for a sign.

And before school, one morning in early December, I got the sign I had been waiting for. The sign that the message I was now sending was being received.

The students were sitting in line, listening to the morning announcements being made by our principal to all of the students at the school. I was in a habit of counting the students each morning, and while doing so, seeing who was and was not at school. Jayden had found a spot at the back of the line where a ray of morning sunlight had crept through the trees and had started to heat the bitumen. I walked past and I heard a 'pssst' next to me.

I looked down and Jayden was positively beaming. What has made this boy so happy today?

'What's up mate?

He whispered, 'Mr Brierley...'

He started to giggle.

'Mr Brierley.'

Yes, mate?

'This morning. When I woke up.'

He put his hands to his mouth so his giggles would not interrupt the principal.

'This morning, I woke up and my arms were made out of chocolate.'

Oh really?

'Yep! So I ate both of them.' And he quickly put his hands to his mouth again to mute the giggles.

Of all the feelings I felt, many of them made my day and week, and even year at that stage. But strangely, one was embarrassment. Stupidly, I realised that my first thought was, 'that can't possibly be true because he still has both his arms'. Despite such obvious stupidity on my part, I finished the year and have continued to teach each year since.

About Nick Brierley

Nick Brierley is an educator advocating for student talents, interests, and needs inspiring classroom practice and using digital technology as an amplifier. Having ten years' experience in primary schools, Nick teaches and coordinates eLearning and Religious Education with students and staff at a primary school on Sydney's north shore. He has completed studies in gifted education, religious education and educational leadership. Nick believes professional learning should be engaging and practical.

Nick is a Google Certified Educator, Google Certified Innovator and has worked with EdTechTeam ANZ to bring Breakout EDU to Australia and New Zealand.

Unforgettable Lessons

Heather Marshall

I have learned many things from my students, from how to "Hit the Qwan" to the correct way to walk in new shoes so that you don't crease them.

The most unforgettable lessons that I have learned weren't taught to me by my most successful students, and have no connection to grades or test scores. I have learned the most from students that would be considered difficult to teach, and these lessons, that were so powerful they changed who I am as a teacher, were the product of relationships.

From my student that had no costume on Halloween, who was glowing with pride as he paraded about in the hand-me-down costume parts I found in my closet, I learned that there is no such thing as a small act of kindness. I also learned that students who are in need of a kind act often won't ask for it; you must listen to these students with your eyes.

As the students were preparing to parade around the school in their costumes, I could tell that he was sad that he had no costume. I had some items in a box in my closet that had been left behind in previous years and we put together a costume. His whole demeanor changed. When I told him he could keep the costume (suspecting he had no costume to wear for trick or treating) he was so happy.

I had several opportunities to show kindness to this student, as he was very much in need. Nothing that I did for him seemed extraordinary to me, but when he moved away the next year I realized just how much all of those little things must have meant to him. He called the school every year to check and see if I was still there and to ask how I was doing. For some of your students, that caring smile and genuine interest in how they are doing may be the only bit of kindness that is afforded to them that day.

The number of years that this student continued to check up on me was a reminder of how powerful my influence is. He taught me that sometimes the most important lessons that you teach cannot be measured by a test score-it's kindness and compassion that leave a lasting impression.

From my student who was "worried about his reputation" I learned to look at my class list in a different way. While reading through the student responses from my favorite back to school activity, I saw the usual worries: grades, homework, not having recess, and then I come across a response that said, "I am worried about my reputation." This from a student that had been in his fair share of trouble in elementary school; and he was right, he did have a reputation that followed him to the middle school.

The next day when I arrived at school he came running across the playground to wish me a good morning. I took the opportunity to let him know that I had read his paper and was confident that his reputation could be whatever he wanted to make it. He ran for student council and became a leader in my class that year. Although he had trouble completing written assignments, when given the opportunity to work on group projects he thrived. He had a great talent for speaking. He was charismatic and entertaining, capturing and holding the attention of his audience. He received high praise from me and his classmates for his energy and creativity, and he began to see himself as we saw him-someone with talent and the potential to influence others.

I am no longer interested in deciding who my students are going to be based on their history. This boy taught me that it is far more important for me to discover which of my students most needs someone to believe in him or her. Which of my students needs someone to see the amazing things that they are capable of, so that they will see it too? Which of my students would like to remake their reputation?

From my student who was late for class more often than he was on time I learned the importance of the statement: "I'm glad you're here." You can't recognize a student's struggles if you don't get to know them-ask questions, and listen-not just with your ears, but with your eyes as well. If you are only focused on their late arrival or whether or not they have their homework, you might miss out on the real accomplishment: that this kid got himself up for school and rode his bike across a bridge during morning rush hour to get here today.

"I'm glad you're here" doesn't mean you have lowered your standards or expectations. In fact, my expectations for this student are much higher because I am expecting him to achieve the same goals, knowing that he is going to have to work twice as hard to get there due to his circumstances. This isn't an "I'm glad you're here and that's all I expect from you for today." It's an "I'm glad you're here, let's do something awesome together today. I'm going to make your struggle to get here mean something. I'm going to make you glad you came."

I look at my students a little differently now because you never know what kind of challenges your kids are facing outside of the classroom. It's because of this student that I am driven to make every day in our classroom worth whatever it took to get there.

In short, my students won't remember my amazing lecture on early river civilizations, or that new technology that we used; they will remember the relationship that we developed, and that in our classroom it felt like a family. They won't remember their standardized test scores or grades; memories are made of feelings. I continue to learn important lessons from the interactions that I have with my students, but if I hadn't gotten to know them and taken an interest in their struggles, I would have missed out on these unforgettable moments.

Don't assume opportunity exists, don't underestimate the impact of kindness and compassion, and most of all, be mindful of your influence-it's powerful and lasting.

About Heather Marshall

Heather's stories span a seventeen year teaching career in both the elementary and middle school settings. The district that she calls home is in the San Francisco Bay Area. It's a unique district, in that it includes only four schools and has a very small town feel to it, while being in a very urban area. She currently teaches an amazing group of kids 6th grade English, World History, and Media Studies.

Somewhere Over the Rainbow

Karen Festa

Someday I'll wish upon a star,
Wake up where the clouds are far behind me
Where trouble melts like lemon drops
High above the chimney top
That's where you'll find me
*Inspired by: Israel Kamakawiwo'ole – Somewhere Over
The Rainbow (lyrics by E.Y. Harburg)

As trouble melts like lemon drops we are here to be your
rainbow...

We've all had moments in the classroom when working with
challenging behaviors.

When all possible tools in our toolbox have been used.
When patience is as thin as dental floss and you've given yourself
a pep talk far too many times to count. Here are 5 reasons why
students with challenging behaviors NEED you:

1. No matter what the behavior is, or how often it occurs,
they need to know you care. Who else would stay up late at night
thinking and reflecting on ways to manage and prevent behavior?
Who else would find the right resources and staff to help guide
them? Who else would greet them at the door each brand new
day with a smile and say, "I'm glad you're here today!"

2. Because you keep in your heart the good days, come
on....you know every student has potential to grow and learn.
Students with challenging behaviors sometimes present them as a

way of communicating. It's our job to dig deeper into the how, when, and why.

3. When all else fails, just sing. I don't have the best singing voice, but I can make any student stop in their tracks just by belting out Taylor Swift's "Shake it off."

4. You are the light at the end of the tunnel. You give hope. You give them purpose. You give them support. Teach them to be confident, set goals, and they CAN make a difference in this world.

5. You have the ability to turn any negative into positives. Every day may not be good, but there's something good in every day. Tell them "YOU MATTER" and believe it. Maybe they already feel the same way about you.

Oh, somewhere over the rainbow way up high
And the dream that you dare to, why, oh why can't I?

About Karen Festa

Karen Festa is a mom of 2 fabulous daughters, a Sunday School teacher and a Special Education teacher at Narragansett Elementary School in Narragansett, Rhode Island. She is a member of the district blended learning committee and the PBIS committee at her school. As an educational consultant for the Rhode Island Department of Education, she presents in various school districts on topics such as; aligning IEP's to CCSS, motivating and engaging all students, and Universal Design for Learning. Karen has co-moderated twitter chats #coteachat, #spedchat, #edbeat, and #udlchat. You can follow her on twitter @teach4spclneeds.

Don't Be Afraid To Get Your Pants Dirty

Kevin M. Cline

I was recently asked by a colleague to list my top 5 "needs" to be an effective teacher. My list: passion, patience, empathy, humility, and love, and I am sure that I saved the biggest for last. It is my ardent belief that every educator must be ready to love every single student from day one. This isn't a passing thought or belief; it is part of my passion for teaching. Having this love for your students pays obvious dividends in classroom planning, quality of activity, excitement of environment, etc., but we cannot forget the role that love for our students plays in effective discipline.

We've all seen the teachers whose idea of effective discipline is to expect abject and thorough obedience, and when that isn't demonstrated by a student, then it's time for a referral and the principal's office. Now, don't get me wrong, I'm all about respect, and certainly realize that there are times when the administrators in the building need to be involved (e.g. fighting, threats, etc.). But so many potential classroom discipline issues can be rendered moot if the student is within a classroom that centers on three fundamental truths- love for the student, fairness of expectation, and mutual respect between the teacher and the student.

I recently finished reading the book *Kids Deserve It!* by Todd Nesloney and Adam Welcome. By the way- If you are an educator or leader in a school, and you're not reading this book, you are missing something special! One chapter of the book was titled "Never Slam the Door", and it spoke to so many of the things on my mind as I work with students. It spoke to the reality of all teachers that we each have had "that student...the one who works to make themself unlovable." I bet that if we all stopped to think about students who have presented the biggest challenges, from a disciplinary angle, this description would likely apply.

So...what do we do with this student? Do we present ourselves as simply another one in a long line of "senders"- teachers dealing with the student by sending them to the office every time a discipline issue arises? Or do we strive to work as a "change agent"- teachers who have decided to try and find the root of these issues, and be an agent of positive influence and change in that student's life? The first route is always an option...if you're looking for the easy way out. But I can assure you, without a doubt in my heart or mind, that this model will not only stunt the growth of a child, but it might also earn you the ire of an administrator. Moreover, it will rob you of an incredible moment of growth that could be had with a student.

I've been very fortunate, over the course of my career, to have had several of these moments with kids. I don't wish for discipline issues, but always try to seize on them as a moment of growth, both for the student and myself. I remember having to write an elaborate classroom management plan while completing my undergraduate work, and emerged from college believing that I needed to have such a plan in place in order to have any kind of order in my classroom. What is clear now, after 12 years of teaching, is that, while it is good to have a process with which one is comfortable, teachers need to be flexible, ready to handle any situation, and ready to understand that each student is going to have a different story, a different need. My process is pretty simple- as a discipline issue arises, I always offer a quick warning (sometimes verbally, sometimes something as simple as moving through the classroom and placing a hand on a shoulder, or a foot to the back leg of the desk). If the issue continues I may ask the student to step outside and have a seat. I know what you're thinking, so far this isn't any different than most teachers. Here is the key, however- never let the situation end there; never "just leave" the student in the hallway.

"That student" for me will always be vividly etched in my memory. This student had a propensity for talking out in class. As often happens, other teachers had felt compelled to "warn" me about this student. Generally I don't listen to such warnings, but I would be lying if I said I wasn't keeping an eye on her. Sure enough, she started the year with issues that ranged from talking out, to sleeping, to being openly defiant. After a warning, I asked her to step outside and have a seat, which she did (with a considerable amount of attitude). The easy way out- claim "good riddance" and be thankful for a few minutes in class without said student. But sitting a student in the hallway does nothing to resolve the issue, and certainly nothing to help the student. As I've written before, it is our responsibility as educators to love every single kid that comes into our classroom, even, and especially so, those that are harder to love than others. I purposely ended class that day with about 5 minutes to spare, and stepped outside into the hallway. The student was sitting down, as I asked her to do, but it was obvious that she was not in a good mood. I sat down beside her, in the hallway, in the dust, and calmly asked her why she believed I had asked her to step out. She explained, perhaps grudgingly, that she had talked out and disrespected me. I then asked her if she thought what I had done in response was fair. The look on her face was priceless. I could tell that she had been expecting detention, and had certainly never been asked that question. She responded with a yes. What then followed was a conversation about the need for mutual respect, and what I believed she could bring to the class and her classmates. By the end of that short 5 minute conversation she was calm, I was calm, and we had an understanding, or at least the beginning of one. And I'm proud to say that, from that moment on, our relationship was one of trust and respect. I continue to look back on that experience as the moment that I began building a relationship of trust and respect with a student for whom I care a great deal.

I share this experience to encourage each of us to remember what Welcome and Nesloney talked about in *Kids Deserve It!* We make nothing better by filling out referral forms left and right; we make no impact on the kids when we fill up detention. Sure, we might gain a day or two of quiet, but how many potential future issues could we solve by simply handling things the right way, the student-centered way, the first time. When confronted with a discipline issue, we have to make the effort to find the root of the issue. We may not know the hurt they are feeling. We may not know how pain in their life is manifesting itself as a discipline problem in school. Give them a chance to talk. "When you listen to a child, you give him back his voice" (Nesloney, 38). This doesn't suggest that one should be lax or stop setting expectations on behavior. It simply means to check your reaction, and make sure that you give the time to a student. Sit with them in the hallway; don't be afraid to get your pants dirty. Treat that student with respect, and don't be shocked when you get it back. Love them...you may be the only one who does.

About Kevin M. Cline

Kevin M. Cline is Department Chair for Social Studies at Frankton High School in Frankton, IN. He can be reached through email at kcline@flcs.k12.in.us and on Twitter @mrclinefhs. Kevin maintains a blog titled "Teaching With Passion" at http://mrclinefhs.blogspot.com/.

How I Became a Curator of ELLStories.com

Ceci Gomez-Galvez

I can confidently say that the birth of ELL Stories came from a tapestry of experiences and borrowed ideas from the most amazing students and teachers anyone could ever have the honor to work with. I am an educator and learner who has learned the most from the power of stories shared by the people that surround me and become part of my own story, and in essence, that is how ELL Stories was born.

As a collaborator, support teacher and passionate cognitive coach, I have been fortunate enough to have a career that allows me to really observe and listen. There is very little work I do in my job that I do on my own. My greatest contributions to education come from collaborations with others, teachers and students alike. I consider myself a constant learner not just because I love being one but because it is an essential part of what I do.

I'll start from the very beginning. In the early days of my teaching career as an EFL (English as a Foreign Language) teacher back in Guatemala, I took many a course on the methodologies of teaching language acquisition. In one such course, I came across a term that has stuck with me over the years: the 'affective filter' (Krashen, 1982) of a language learner. This filter refers to the emotional influence towards learning a language and whether it affects the input and learning. Within its hypothesis, it asks the question: Can someone acquire a second/foreign language if they're not emotionally open to doing so? The answer is not as simple as one might think. The language can in fact be learned even if the student resists it. The power of acquisition of language and need for communication surpasses any emotional resistance we might have to it. For instance, when I moved to Italy in 2010, I had a real hard time acculturating to the fast-paced, industrially-minded Milanese lifestyle. For the first three years I lived, worked and was immersed in an (almost exclusively) Italian speaking community; yes, I of course learned it. I figured things out and made connections. I learned how to read it, how to hear it, and how to apply it when necessary. However I didn't identify with it as my own and by applying my 'affective filter', my only goal was to use it only if and when I needed to. So, could I have read a poem in Italian and understood its meaning? Yes. Could I have written my own poetry in Italian to convey a personal message about myself? I don't believe so, but then again, I didn't try. I wouldn't have thought of expressing myself creatively or personally in a language I didn't identify with. I was living proof of the 'affective filter' I had learned about so many years prior.

When I started working in the international school setting, my role from language acquisition specialist started taking shape to more of a coaching role, a guide for English language learners to apply the language they were learning in a powerful way. That's when I started wondering to what extent an ELL learns to communicate in English. When tasked to write personal pieces, powerful poetry or give speeches about something they were passionate about; how could I guide ELLs into doing that, finding their own identities and voice in a language that wasn't their first?

Three years ago, I had the wonderful opportunity to co-teach a creative writing class. Without realizing it at the time, co-teaching this class with my teaching partner and coaching mentor Nathan Lill was going to change my approach to language teaching. It was then that I started focusing my support on empowering ELLs to apply English as a form of communication beyond just their academic requirements. All writers in our class were given the opportunities to explore their writing skills and various forms or writing, without fear. We created a writing community with a digital repository of writing, digital writer portfolios to showcase them as authors of their work and end-of-semester publishing celebrations where writers shared their beautiful powerful pieces to an audience of teachers, parents and their peers. As their writing teacher and to model the writing process, it was then that I began to also find my own voice and identity in a language I had only used professionally until that point.

At this same time, I was supporting middle school students and also co-teaching with Nathan and Rosana Walsh, as we strived to strengthen a literacy rich Humanities curriculum. While the seed of empowering ELLs had been planted in the creative writing class, it wasn't until we co-created the 'This I Believe' Podcast project for grade eight students that I understood the power of personal narratives and the importance of making such opportunities for ELLs and all students.

In the past three years, co-creating projects of this caliber with Nathan, Rosana and other amazing educators; as well as working with ELLs with whom I started building strong bonds; nurtured the seed that was planted in the writing class. We were unknowingly becoming part of our ELLs' stories of finding their identity and voices in English. The opportunities they were having to connect with the language were having a direct impact on them not just as learners but as human beings. ELL Stories were being lived and experienced right before us, waiting to be told.

In my journey as an educator, I have found incredible value in creating digital spaces to curate student work. Looking for ways our learners can have authentic audiences with whom they can share their work, creates a sense of personal connection to their daily learning. For instance, instead of a writing piece turned in for grading, living a short life from creation to completion; I want students to feel their work has meaning beyond the grade they receive. That their connection to the work they do defines them as more than learners, but that it starts to define the quality of who they're becoming as citizens of the world. This being a mindset, knowing these spaces to be effective in that purpose, it only took a five minute conversation with an educator and coach I admire greatly, Shaun Kirkwood, whose innovative ideas on how to make learning accessible and fun for all, showed me the space he's created to share his ideas with the world. His digital space screams "Take these strategies! Use them with your learners! Have fun and make them your own!" and in truth, it's one of the humblest approaches to the deprivatization of good practices I have ever witnessed. All I could think was: I want to be like Shaun. I want to create not own, a space that has a positive impact in anyone who contributes to it and the people who use its content. I was inspired.

This past year, I was given the opportunity to tell a personal story, out loud, in a room full of people. In English. It was quite possibly one of the most vulnerable, nerve-racking and, well, necessary things I have ever done as an ELL. I could not thank Trey Hobbs and his Shenzhen Stories initiative more for giving me the opportunity to dig deep into my experiences and gather the courage to tell them. It was a beautiful and important moment for me as person, not just a language learner and teacher. It made me wonder what stories from ELLs we have not heard that would need a similar stage. Inspired by this experience, Trey and I talked about organizing a student-led event where we would create that space for our learners. The idea was great, the timing was not, and we weren't able to get traction on our project. But thanks to this, the seed that had been planted long ago in the writing class was growing roots.

You can see how ELL Stories started to come together, all the pieces falling into place. For years now I have unknowingly been putting together this puzzle, but it hadn't become clear what the pieces were forming. And like any good puzzle, there's that moment when the last piece is left which ties it all together to form a whole. This last piece fell into place when I read one of the most powerful ELL Stories I have ever heard. Reading Emily Francis' "New Land, New Opportunity" solidified my desire to continue to empower ELLs to find their voice and be brave enough to share their journeys as bilinguals, as learners, as people. The power in Emily's story about her family and her migration to the United States from Guatemala, the sacrifices and hardships that defined her world for a long time, and her resilience to overcome them to be where she is today was the definitive moment where I knew I must create a space for more stories to be told.

The seed, its roots; something sprouted. Something grew out of the ground. The puzzle complete. ELL Stories was born.

About Ceci Gomez-Galvez

Originally from Guatemala, Ceci has worked at international schools back home, Italy and now China. Her career as an ELL specialist has evolved into many forms. Right now, she's the leader of an ELL support program based on support practices within a sheltered immersion philosophy and the use of differentiation strategies at Shekou International School (#sisrocks). She's a collaborator, consultant and coach who empowers educators to create learning opportunities to suit all language learners' needs, and an innovator who effectively integrates eLearning tools and the practice of 21st century skills to enhance learning for ELLs and all students.

I don't know. Can you?

Amanda Casto

I have many dreams for my students. I want them to be critical thinkers, life-long learners, and passionate individuals. I want them to realize their potential and maintain a growth mindset. I want them to recognize the importance of due dates and deadlines. I want them to always be prepared with paper and a pencil (I am a needy math teacher...what can I say?) I want them to stand up to bullies, stand up to each other, and stand up for what is right. I want them to move mountains. I want them, at any cost, to choose kind.

This list is never-ending. However, it begins with the single greatest aspiration I have for all of my students: Respect.

Respect...a sometimes frustrating concept to teach middle schoolers. They are at a critical point in their development where their patience is low in supply and their demand is high. They live in an age of instant gratification and presume they know the answer before they even ask the question. It is hard to be a pre-teen let alone a pre-teen with manners.

I employ many classroom procedures and rules which require respect. Don't talk when others are talking, say "please" when you ask for something and "thank you" when you receive it, when going into the cafeteria, hold the door for the person behind you, etc. This is second-nature for most of my students and usually it only takes one or two weeks in August to retrain these habits. That being said, there is one habit that takes an entire school year to teach. This lesson happens multiple times a day with a handful of students. It is a lesson that I teach several times each whenever the question is asked, "Can I go to the bathroom?"

I dread this question. Even with a systematic sign-in and sign-out procedure, students still ask me this question. Who knew that a string of six simple words could make me want to tear my hair out? These words flow from the lips of at least 10% of my classes on a daily basis. Even when I banned this question from my classroom in the past, students still seem to squeeze it into their daily vernacular. They just can't seem to help themselves from asking this question!

Why is this question so lousy? It may not be the reason you think. You see, I feel that two things carry you far in this world: manners and a smile. Manners are so important yet they have been overlooked in today's society as an integral skill that all respectful people have. Manners are at the top of my lesson plan. I may not inspire my students to major in mathematics someday and some of them won't ever understand the formula of finding the area of a circle; however, they will walk out of my classroom with an appreciation for having good manners. For example, any of them will tell you that "please" and "thank you" are non-negotiables in my classroom. They know that I believe using proper manners could simply place you on someone's "good side," get you that second date, or even make or break an interview. Manners matter. Which is the reason why I loathe that specific question. As simple as it is, it lacks manners.

So when my students approach me with that dreaded question, I reply, "I don't know. Can you?" My question makes them think about the context of what they are truly asking. It may take a couple of days, a few weeks, or an entire school year; eventually, they ask the correct question,

"May I please go the bathroom."

And I reply with a smile, "Yes. Yes, you may."

Ask any of my students if you can know one of their teacher's most popular catchphrases, and they will respond, "I don't know. Can you?"

About Amanda Casto

Amanda is a middle school teacher and Ph.D. student at the University of North Carolina at Charlotte. She has over ten years of teaching experience in grades K-8. During her "free time", she enjoys tweeting with other educators, reading YA literature, watching baseball, and traveling with her husband, Brian.

The Hilda Rule

Amy Gorzynski

Teachers do things all day every day and never realize their reach. That's exactly how I would describe the moment that would potentially change the path of one of my students, and my path too.

A couple years ago I started a student organization at my high school called the TechgURLs. The mission of the club is "to expose girls to the options that are out there in the field of technology and provide opportunities and experiences to learn more about it". As the club sponsor, I am always looking for opportunities for the girls to explore technology, develop skills and build their personal learning network (PLN). During winter break of the 2014-15 school year, I found out that Girls Who Code (GWC), a national organization that hosts programs around the country from Los Angeles to New York, was coming to Chicago to run their summer immersion program.

TechgURLs was still fairly new and I was still getting to know the girls, but I passed out information on the Girls Who Code summer program to my girls at a club meeting in January not knowing if anyone would be interested. Unbeknownst to me, a sophomore named Hilda filled out the application, and was put on the waitlist. That April she received an email from GWC explaining that she had been removed from the waitlist and a spot was available for her. So, imagine my surprise when she walked into my office the next morning and said that she needed to accept the invitation and complete the registration form within 24 hours! She was freaking out...I was freaking out...and rightfully so. We both understood the magnitude of this opportunity. But, Hilda also knew there were a lot of obstacles in her way, and the logistics of it all made her hesitate. First, there was a transportation issue. Hilda lived in Melrose Park, a suburb of Chicago, and the program was downtown. Saying yes to this opportunity meant that she would have to take 2 buses, 1 train and walk over a mile every morning and every afternoon for six weeks. Not only would that cost money, but it also required parent permission. On top of that, the program ended in late August, and Hilda would have to miss the first 2 weeks of school.

It was a HUGE risk.

Funny enough, when I looked at this girl, who had just come from Mexico a couple years before, who was still learning English, and thought about all of these obstacles, the word "No" never crossed my mind. I told Hilda to submit the registration form and we'd worry about it later. So she took the risk, and with the help of the building principal, Jason Markey, we figured it out.

Hilda worked hard that summer, and the Girls Who Code Summer Immersion Program proved to be life-changing for her. Aside from the multiple coding languages she learned, she made valuable connections with fellow classmates, instructors and professionals in the industry. She had the opportunity to showcase her work in exhibition at the end of the program, and receive feedback from engineers and computer scientists from Groupon and the like. The experience also solidified her interest in pursuing a career in technology.

The next school year, as a result of her time spent at the GWC, Mr. Markey asked both Hilda and me to join him in co-keynoting the EdTech Summit Featuring Google for Education in Montreal! The title of his keynote was "Chance Favors the

Connected School" and he wanted us to tell our story. We gladly accepted and in April 2016 we made our international debut!

As I nervously awaited my turn at the podium, I reflected on the year's events that led to that very moment. I thought about the purpose of our keynote - to encourage educators to reach out and connect with people outside of their school building - and how those connections add value to the learning process. Hilda, wise beyond her years, embodied that message in everything she did. I thought about myself at her age, the opportunities that existed when I was in high school, and why those conversations were fleeting and messages rarely received. I learned a lot from Hilda along the way, but two lessons stand out. 1. Take risks and get out of your comfort zone. And, 2. Never underestimate the power of relationships because a positive connection can turn those seemingly small moments and insignificant conversations into something big. Even more, this experience has reminded me that there are a lot of "Hildas" out there and it's so important to seek out opportunities to get to know my students on a deeper level.

I couldn't help but beam with pride as I watched her on stage, retelling her story to hundreds of teachers and administrators from The United States and Canada. After she finished, the crowd exploded into applause. She killed it. Dozens of audience members sought her out that day to congratulate her or share their own story. While many distinguished educators led workshops on technology tools and innovative teaching practices that weekend, Hilda was easily the star of the conference.

Attending the Montreal Summit ignited something in both of us, and prompted Hilda to "pay it forward" in a big way. She decided her next logical step was to host a technology summit back home for students in 4-8th grade. Her goal was to get more kids interested in technology at a younger age, and help them realize that technology is everywhere, and it doesn't have to be intimidating or scary. She wanted to provide them with an opportunity to take a risk like she did. Even better, she enlisted the help of her classmates to get it done!

In five weeks, Hilda organized the entire event - from making the schedule and recruiting high school students to run the workshops, to making promotional posters and launching a social media campaign to advertise the event to the community. On June 17, 2016, 120 students attended the inaugural Leyden Student Summit and attended workshops on robotics, digital electronics, coding, fashion design, digital footprint, image editing, animation, Breakout EDU and digital storytelling. The feedback we received from both the attendees and their parent was overwhelmingly positive and we knew the event was a success. Being a part of something like that always feels good, but taking a step back and watching Hilda take the reins will always be one of my proudest moments as a teacher.

Hilda's story is serendipitous, to say the least. Who could have predicted that handing out a simple piece of paper would have such far-reaching the effects? When I think back to the day Hilda walked into my office to figure out how to make the Girls Who Code opportunity a reality, it still blows my mind. Most kids would have looked at that list of obstacles and said "forget it". But the difference between most kids and Hilda is that she saw the big picture. She knew the impact this could have on her future, and she reached out. Then, she took her experiences and turned them into an opportunity for hundreds more.

Some might see her as the exception to the rule. But what if Hilda's story was the rule? What if we as educators took more risks and took more time to consider possibilities without limitations, just like Hilda?

About Amy Gorzynski

Amy Gorzynski obtained her BA in Business Administration from Illinois Wesleyan University in 2002 and MA in Secondary Ed (Business Education) from Roosevelt University in 2004. She has been a full-time Business & Technology teacher at Leyden High Schools (#212) since 2004. She earned her CAS in Curriculum & Instruction, with an ESL endorsement from National Louis University in 2015. She has taught courses in Digital Literacy, Social Media, Entrepreneurship, Consumer Ed and Web Design. In addition to teaching, she sponsors the school's TechgURLs club. She understands the need for more female representation in the tech industry and works to provide opportunities that will encourage and inspire more girls to consider this ever-changing and rapidly expanding career path.

Building a Community Environment that Has Lasting Impact

Ixchell Reyes

"Teacher, teacher!" In the Chinese, Japanese, Korean, Arabic cultures to name a few, the teaching profession is one of the most esteemed roles in the community, and individuals show respect by never addressing a teacher by their name, for that would be reproachable. This notion contradicts the American individualist thought that we are all different and unique; and names are extremely important. To that end, I have heard many instructors become annoyed and respond with "Yes, student?" rather than taking a few minutes to explain this concept at the beginning of class. Something seemingly simple as how to address a teacher is cultural and teachers should take time to explain this at the beginning of every term. That said, "teacher, teacher!" warms my heart, for it refers to what I do, teach.

Working with international populations of students preparing to complete a degree in America is a privilege. I have absorbed the culture of my students without having to travel. A teacher's salary is barely enough to make a living in a big city, so every time I learn something new, I cherish the experience.

I am a high-energy teacher, and I am a firm believer in modeling a positive attitude toward life, learning, and language. This means that even on difficult mornings, I walk into my classroom ready to tackle whatever that day has in store for my class. No matter what is on our agenda, it is important to spend some time connecting with students that are more susceptible to homesickness or culture clash as they adjust in America on their first weeks.

For fourteen weeks, nine hours per week, I help my students build a classroom environment of community, especially since they often lean on each other for support as they adjust to living in another country. Personal support groups are incredibly powerful, and neither teachers nor students often realize that. Thus, the fourteen weeks we spend together provide me with the opportunity to help students become acclimated to the target culture so their transition into an American university is smooth and successful.

One thing my students learn is that there is no other way I would rather spend my early mornings than working with them. Therefore, I expect as much enthusiasm from them as possible. At 8am, my students are sleepy, often because they've stayed up studying for the GRE or Skyping with their families, so their enthusiasm might need a little prompting. Before walking into the room, I always take a deep breath, open the door with a smile, and start class with some kind of greeting.

This spring, it was, "Good morning, sunshines!"

Every morning, for fourteen weeks, my students would wait for the latecomers to arrive and over time, their reaction would show appreciation for the tardy student, "the sunshine is here!" Such a simple action, a verbal acknowledgement that someone we consider part of our in-group has arrived acted as a reinforcement for that environment of community that we worked to build. Picture in your mind a room full of adult students, engineers, all struggling to make sense of American customs, culture, and norms. That simple greeting served as a routine that started every class session with an unspoken promise that both me and my students would try our best to cope with whatever life or school flings in our direction. It became our morning ritual.

This particular semester, the majority of my students were Mandarin speakers, which made it harder for them to force themselves to speak English in the classroom. However, very quickly, I noticed they took pride in greeting each other with what they now knew was the special phrase in our class, "Good morning, sunshine!" This is true for every student except for one who was visibly nervous every time he had to speak. He would speak softly and blush every time. He would stumble on words whenever I walked over to him. It was clear that the spotlight would cause him anxiety. I worried that this would get in the way of his opportunities to practice English, and I spent a lot of time making sure I had less-stressful chances for him to share with others in small groups. But I was never completely satisfied or sure that my attempts were working.

Until midterm self-evaluations.

This brings me to another crucial skill that I stress practicing in all that we do, self-reflection. At midterm, I ask students to reflect on the challenges they've overcome, the goals they set for themselves, and what they have learned. They are to record a video only viewable to me and summarize their reflection. On my train commute to the campus, I watch their responses and give them feedback or encouragement. The last entry was from my super-shy student. His narration was organized, and connected, as usual. He appreciated the grammar structures I had taught them, and he had challenged himself to practice English more and to learn more GRE vocabulary. Typical comments. Until I came to the last few seconds of the recording.

"This semester, I am happy because you helped make the class very comfortable for us. You give us games and make it easy for Chinese students to pay attention to the class. Ms. Ixchell, you are the sunshine." My eyes welled up because for this student, being able to share and speak in class was so difficult, yet in this short video, he expressed himself so eloquently and offered praise for our accepting class environment. Little did he realize that all of us together created that environment. And little did I realize that every morning, our ritual was something he paid attention to!

This was a testimony of how the little things we sometimes overlook can have a deep impact on students. The term ended a few weeks ago, and saying goodbye to my students is always bittersweet because we become a little family that helps one another, groans at the tests and quizzes, learns to adapt to American academic expectations and behavior, and enjoys each other's company and celebrates diversity. And though my sunshines have learned to address me by my name, they still playfully call me, "teacher."

About Ixchell Reyes

Ixchell is an ESL instructor at the University of Southern California's International Academy, where she teaches graduate students. Her knowledge of foreign languages and experience teaching abroad helps her to connect with students who arrive in America to complete a university degree. Her areas of passion are teaching graduate writing and tinkering with educational technology. She likes pushing boundaries and teaching students that they can effect change by channeling their talent.

Triangle of Trust

Marilyn McAlister

I've been teaching for 24 years now. I've learned a lot over the years. But the biggest lesson I learned was 20 years ago. I know it was 20 years ago because my precious daughter is 20 and she is part of the story. Here it is:

I was a young mother and teacher. I had a loving husband and had just started working at a new school. Our careers and lives were on the right path. Our pastor's wife was raising children of her own and had happily agreed to watch our baby while we were at work.

So what was the problem? I knew our daughter was in caring hands. I knew the babysitter had a nurturing environment. I even knew that the babysitter loved our daughter like one of her own. The problem: I was tremendously jealous of the babysitter.

I would cry at night feeling guilty for having to leave our baby. I would cry because I felt like someone else was raising our baby. My husband comforted and counseled, but I still cried and was still filled with jealousy and guilt.

One day, I shared my feelings with a dear friend. (I call her Peace, she calls me Joy.) I shared how I was jealous of the love the babysitter had for our daughter. She just shook her head and laughed. "Marilyn," she said, "that's exactly what you want. How blessed is she (my daughter) to have someone love her that much." That hit home. My friend was right. I was being selfish thinking that we, her parents, were the only ones to love her. I should look at it as a privilege that others would love her like we do.

This was my lesson. There is a triangle of trust that comes into play. Just as I left my daughter in the care of the babysitter, my students' parents were sending their children to me. In essence, I was like the babysitter that was spending the day with their children. These parents were trusting me to educate, nurture, and love them, just like I was trusting the babysitter.

Twenty years later, this is still the biggest lesson I've learned as an educator. Academics are important, but the relationship with our students and their parents are even more important. We are entrusted with precious children. Let's treat them like our own. John 13:34 tells us to "Love one another." Let's make it our goal, daily, to do just that.

PS: When we had our second child, my friend became our son's babysitter.

About Marilyn McAlister

Marilyn is a 6th grade teacher in the Imperial Valley, California. An educator for 24 years, she's passionate about building relationships with her students and their parents. The daughter in her story is attending college to become a teacher. With love and encouragement, our children and students will succeed.

Making an Impact - One Student at a Time

Dan Popescu and Mohamad Srour

The genesis of our relationship began in 7th grade - a time when I was merely a name among the rest of my peers, indistinguishable and without a strong personality. What made my situation worse was the attitude of acceptance I had adopted about my status. I could not fathom that I had the potential to be someone who my peers would someday look up to and respect as a superior student athlete. Mr. Dan was my Physical Education teacher when he first noticed that there was more to me than what most people saw. We were swimming that day and I was struggling to make it from one end of the pool to the other. I had no technique so the most that I could do was flap my arms and kick violently, hoping that I would make it to the other side without drowning and subsequently embarrassing myself in front of my classmates. All that I had was my determination, which Mr. Dan saw and for some reason decided to nurture. He approached me after class and made me a proposition I never would have expected - "You might want to try Swimming Club on Monday after school. I want to see you there."

If I had more self-confidence at the time, I would have declined his offer, but I found myself in an awkward situation in which I felt compelled to accept. I dreaded my decision every day leading up to that first practice, wishing that Mr. Dan wasn't my PE teacher so that I could get away with not going more easily. I was an amateur compared to everyone else, and initially I felt that I would never catch up to them. At the end of that swim session, however, I left practice with a renewed sense of hope. What made the difference was the constant supply of encouragement I received from Mr. Dan, who made me feel as though I deserved to be there. Rather than reprimand me in anger for making a mistake, he corrected me with patience and made me try the stroke again until I executed it perfectly. I appreciated that aspect of his guidance the most.

Under Mr. Dan's tutelage, my rise was meteoric. In the space of a year, I went from the new kid on the block, with no skills or experience, to one of the only swimmers who won both races at any of his competitions. I continued to evolve from that point onwards and the following year I received my first regional silver medal, competing against swimmers from all over the world. This success endowed me with a self-confidence that allowed me to pursue greatness in other facets of my high school career. By tenth grade, I was the deputy head of the Student Life Organization, a well-respected position among the student body that raised my self-esteem and self-respect, encouraging me to make a positive impact on my community. I had also branched out into other sports such as soccer, basketball, and track and field, excelling at each and achieving comparable success.

Throughout this period of growth and success, my relationship with Mr. Dan also evolved, transforming from a mere student-teacher relationship devoid of emotional attachment to a friendship characterized by trust and mutual respect. When I became captain of the swim team, he often made me lead practices, and I later realized that he did so because he believed that I could push others in the same way he pushed me. I also noticed that he no longer challenged me as he did before, possibly because he recognized that I had become self-motivated and could challenge myself. His job was done and it was my time to take over what he started five years ago on that fateful Monday.

When we parted ways, I knew that I would miss his presence in my life, but I was not at all worried that my personal development would cease after that point. Even though he was gone, the principles he had instilled in me were not. He unearthed a fighter, one who now believes that with enough hard work and perseverance, any adversity can be overcome and any dream can be fulfilled.

These are some paragraphs written by one of my former students, Mohamad Srour, as part of his University's application process. Currently Mohamad is studying at Boston University Dental School. He is on his journey to become an amazing dentist, perhaps inspired by his father's success in this field. I wanted to share his own words, because I haven't realized the deep impact I had on Mohamad, until his writing came two years after my departure from Al Ain. During my four years there, I was his PE teacher and Coach for swimming, basketball, softball, cross country and track & field.

How can we measure the impact we have daily on our students? Can we even measure it accurately? What is the real number of students that are significantly impacted in a positive way by our teaching? How do we as teachers know we have done enough for our students to inspire them in becoming whatever they want, wherever they find true passion? All these questions are coming into my head every time I am reflecting on my teaching practices and philosophy.

Going back to Mohamad's words, I realized at the time that I have inspired and nurtured great qualities in him, but had no idea how deep and meaningful the impact was. When he shared the university application letter with me, I was extremely moved and it got me to reflect more on my teaching practices and approaches to building positive teacher-student relationships. Maybe we don't realize, but in some cases, we, the teachers, are the only rays of sunshine in our students' lives.

I truly believe that it is significantly more important and relevant to establish a harmonious relationship between us and students prior to content teaching. If they like us, they will learn. Looking back to my time in school, even to this day I can remember every teacher or coach that impacted my life and the journey I embarked as an international educator. Fortunately or unfortunately, there is no neutral impact; through our teaching we always leave a mark on our students, whether it is positive or negative. In every lesson and every coaching session, we have the opportunity to make a difference in their lives; it had better be a significant one.

I have been fortunate to get into this wonderful world of international education and meet amazing students and teachers along the way that keep me inspired every day. My journey has its own challenges, but it's very rewarding. There is no better moment than the one when I am in front of my students. This gives me daily opportunities to make a positive impact in their lives.

About Dan Popescu

Dan is a Romanian citizen, and studied in Romania before moving to the United States for a non-teaching position. In 2010, he started his career as PE teacher in United Arab Emirates. After few years there, he moved in China where he currently teaches. This summer he is back on the road moving to Bangladesh for another professional challenge. He is a passionate educator, traveler and learner. He has experience with primary and secondary students; his favorite approach to teaching and learning is inquiry based and game sense.

About Mohamad Srour

Mohamad is a Syrian citizen. He spent most of his time studying in United Arab Emirates. Currently he is a student at Boston University Dental School pursuing a career in dentistry.

He is very passionate about sports and became quite skilled in a variety of disciplines like swimming, basketball, football and track & fielding. He is fortunate to have an amazing and very supportive family. Mr. Dan was one of his impact teachers that inspired him to dream big and pursue his goals.

They Are All "Our" Kids

Heather Green

I recently read "It's increasingly difficult to live in a nation that reveres pulling one's self up by the bootstraps when you don't have any bootstraps." That is a sentiment that resonates with me in giant, gong-banging fashion, especially after spending time in both social service and public education careers. It's mind-numbingly simplistic to categorically dismiss challenging students, delinquent students, severe classroom disrupters, or so-called neighborhood menaces as lost causes. But make no mistake, they are still very much children. And whether you are an educator in a public or private school, a single and childless professional, or a retired doctor with grandchildren, all kids are our kids. The current generation of school aged children comprise our nation's future economic, social, and political portrait. "Our job is to teach the students we have. Not the ones we would like to have. Not the ones we used to have. Those we have right now. All of them." - Dr. Kevin Maxwell

In the spirit of transparency, I haven't always "gotten" this sentiment, the idea that to truly make a difference, I've got to at times put aside societal expectations of how kids "should" act in a classroom. High expectations are necessary, but rigidity will hastily get even the best teacher painted into a corner. I haven't always possessed the understanding that only classroom experience brings: that even the soundest educational pedagogy paving the way to successful standardized assessment data results has to, at times, be placed secondary in importance to a child's emotional, nutritional, and social needs. One of my most challenging students, hearkening back to my first year in the classroom, had me convinced that I was doing everything right, it was the child who was the problem. I gave up on him. I focused on his classmates who were eager to learn, respectful, and admittedly, easier to teach.

Reflecting on situations like I described, I've learned a few keys for success with each kid. One, success does not look the same on each student. What is growth for one child looks completely different than growth for another child, even within the same classroom. Two, pardon the cliche, but fair is not equal. Fair means I provide each child with what they individually need. Lastly, I must approach each child with empathy for whatever their home life may be like, empathy for however their morning may have started, and empathy for the fact that, honestly, being a kid is often difficult. I've experienced that incorporating these mindsets into my classroom leads to success. But, my definition of success is different for each child. Isn't that what's considered personalized instruction, the ideal we're endeavoring toward in education?

One recent year I taught a child who has been in and out of juvenile hall, alternative school, and back to public school again, like a revolving door. Candace had a clinical addiction to at least two illegal drugs, as well as a known history of distributing illegal substances. This child was thirteen. First or second year teacher self would have been steadfast in my high expectations for classroom engagement, "no excuses!" But instead, I approached Candace with an individualized plan for success, an understanding of her needs she brought to the class that neither of us could control, and, most importantly, I approached her with empathy. Consequently, while Candace missed quite a bit of my class, the time that she did spend with me was largely free of discord, free of disruption to other learners, and she walked away from my class with new skills in the content area. Growth is growth. A successful day for one child cannot be measured against a successful day for the next child.

Teaching anywhere brings challenges and the results of home life, for good or not, are evident in schools. The school I call my professional home is a typical Title 1 campus, if you double the percentage which qualifies a school to receive Title 1 funding. With low socio-economic children come academic and social challenges that might not be as prevalent in non-Title 1 schools. There are a host of characteristics that children from poverty bring to school that aren't necessarily evaluated or taught in classic university teacher colleges, or even alternative teacher certification programs. How does a teacher approach a child who is perpetually with a headache at school because they don't get adequate meals at home? What about the child with clinical depression who doesn't have access to mental health care? Or, the child who is emotionally fragile at school after seeing his parent murdered? While it's true that these situations can arise in any home, children in poverty have far fewer coping skills and support resources available. My student Candace brought a host of challenges to the classroom that I was, if I'm being brutally honest, ill-equipped to solve. But a true teacher is also a master problem solver, and while I could not solve the root problems Candace brought to my class, I could problem solve to minimize her distraction to her peers and maximize to the best extent possible her experiences within my classroom.

According to a federal report from the Southern Education Foundation, 51% of American public school children in 2013 were considered low-income and/or were eligible for free and reduced lunch programming. That number is increasing. Children emulate what they see and in the case of my student Candace, she followed in the footsteps of a chemically dependent single parent and picked up unhealthy social habits from examples she saw in her neighborhood. The work of Eric Jensen among others has provided detailed insight into how a "brain on poverty" functions versus a healthy, middle class, well-nurtured and cared for brain. In the ever-widening gap between the haves (intact families, food security, access to healthcare, early childhood learning, pre-kinder vocabulary development, and adult literacy in the home) versus the have-nots, the classroom is not a level playing field from the moment a child begins their k-12 career. Access to quality pre-k programming can benefit children in poverty, but it is not a silver bullet.

Ruby Payne has taught scores of educators over twenty years about the differences between a poverty mindset and a middle class mindset. The poverty mindset is one that many, dare I say most, adults with a middle class mindset cannot relate to. In addition to sound nutrition, exposure to words (both quality and quantity), and functional households, many children from middle school settings arrive at school with a future-driven, goal-setting, and professional and/or collegiate aspiring thought process. Candace presented with a smorgasbord of barriers even outside of being a product of poverty and having a drug addiction: she read well below grade level, her social skills were underdeveloped, and the school counselor suspected she was emotionally disturbed - but her parent did not provide consent for her to be evaluated for special education service eligibility. Children from poverty are not only often lacking in Maslow's basics, but also have little to zero exposure to long-term planning or the simple yet incredibly important piece of development known as hope. Hope for more, for better, hope for a successful future.

Academically, children from poverty hold large word gaps, exhibit lagging reading skills, and possess very short-term idea of their future. They are kids who frequently have weak social skills and can be emotionally volatile. These characteristics can play out in the classroom as lack of interest in lessons and learning, disruptive conduct, and frequent visits to the principal's office or even alternative school placement. Not only does a child living in extreme poverty present in classrooms with lagging academic growth compared to middle class peers, the gaps widen with each time out of the classroom, each suspension, and each summer where zero learning (and even regression, summer slide) occurs. How can I expect the student in my second period who is homeless, who missed the city bus that picks him up from his shelter, subsequently missing school-provided breakfast (his only option for breakfast), to be enthusiastically engaged in my creative/amazing/fun (in my mind) lesson on plate tectonics? This is the same child who reads two to three grade levels behind his peers, is projected as high-risk for dropping out of high school, and - bonus - he knows of these labels assigned to him.

My student Candace defied at least one odd and left middle school to enter high school. Her troubles, of course, followed her into ninth grade, so a high school social worker took her under her wing and guided her into a "second chance" high school where Candace would receive more one to one guidance and instruction. While Candace did not earn her traditional high school diploma, she did receive her General Equivalency Diploma and is now working full time, supporting herself and her three year old son. I won't posture that I was some lynchpin for Candace, but I was responsible for my spoke in the wheel of her upbringing. I teach for all students, but I wholly recognize that my heart, moral compass, and service is pulled toward those children who need positive adult interaction and competent teaching the very most. I say this often and I sincerely mean it, "If not me (us), then who?"

When I observe students in schools, the ones considered hardest to reach and support, I often wonder, "What's happened? Who are they modeling?" There's a tendency, even among some of the most dedicated and passionate educators, to place an inordinate degree of focus on students that are the most challenging, the most difficult. But, the old teaching adage, "We spend 90% of our time on 10% of students," is supremely accurate. At some schools, that 10% is even lower. But they are all, each, our students, our kids. They each represent a potential success story, a scientist, a peace-maker, a nurse, a firefighter, an engineer for public good, or the next generation of educators.

Teaching is increasingly challenging, demanding, and emotionally consuming. But, conversely, it's uplifting, joyful, and a virtual bear hug many times throughout a day. Many, if not most, students are "easier" to teach than our proverbial 10%. They are more enjoyable, funnier, more literate, and arrive at school better equipped to learn. However, find me a teacher who is only in the profession for the "easy" kids and I'll show you a teacher who doesn't grasp the critical nature of the mission. One of my favorite Twitterers recently said it best:

Amy Fast, Ed.D
@fastcranny

The hardest thing about being an educator is facing the reality you can't save every kid while holding onto the unshakable hope that you can

RETWEETS LIKES
167   393

7:13 PM - 13 Mar 2017

7   167   393

This is why I teach. The mission. The need for a positive impact for all of our kids.

(Names, ages, genders, and some factors have been edited to protect student privacy.)

About Heather Green

Heather currently serves in a hybrid, teacher & campus leader, role at a Title 1 middle school near Dallas, TX. She's taught science, AVID, and technology applications. Currently, she writes the social-emotional learning lessons for her campus. Heather was first a youth social services provider and then by accident, yet happily, found herself recruited into the classroom. Heather embraces an "each one teach one" mentality in her classroom and expects to learn as much from her students as they do from her. You can find her Tweeting often, with never-ending attempts at largely unsuccessful comedy, @SassyTeaching.

Afterword

"Five card stud, nothing wild. And the sky's the limit"
- Captain Jean Luc Picard, *Star Trek: The Next Generation*

Thank you. Thank you for reading. Thank you for being part of these incredible stories.

It all started as a simple 20Time Project, and grew to a real passion project.

As with any 20Time Project, how do you evaluate if you were successful? Can you assign a grade to this work? In all honesty, I won't be able to evaluate this success until after publication. I have to wait and watch the ripples grow. And just like teaching, I may never know the full impact of this collection of stories.

If a story or this collection has impacted you in any way, please share on Twitter using #FBCALbook.

Overall, I'm amazed at how many people rallied up support for this project. There was a great deal of excitement, with over 120 people interested in writing, 53 who submitted stories, and many people who offered to help with editing.

Who knows, maybe someday there will be a Fueled by Coffee and Love, Volume 2?

Acknowledgements

This project wouldn't have come together without the help of so many amazing friends.

A huge shoutout to Aubrey Yeh, who has been involved since before this was even an idea--thank you for believing in the power of sharing stories, encouraging this project the whole way, and working on all the major and minor editing details. Thank you Nick Brierley for being an incredible cheerleader for this project and for providing feedback and edits at all the key steps. Thank you Meagan Kelly for going above and beyond to help with final edits. Hugs and thanks to Michele Osinski for designing and creating the FBCAL logo, and for your hard work creating the beautiful cover design.

Thank you Chris Craft for being an amazing mentor and friend, and for pushing me beyond what I think I can do. You're the best! Thank you Jennie Magiera for inspiring us to share our teacher stories in your ISTE 2017 keynote; I'm grateful you're my #COL16 coach, and #TeamYoshi leader. Thank you Jess Loucks, for teaching me to "yes, and" and dream big.

Thank you Sarah Thomas, for hearing my initial ideas, and sharing resources to help me get started. Thank you to Doug Robertson for bouncing around ideas, guiding me in the right direction with publishing, and for volunteering to write the introduction. Thank you Brian Costello for providing great publishing tips and project encouragement.

Thank you Ray Charbonneau, for helping me with the formatting, prepping, and publishing. (Check out his website for more: www.y42k.com.)

Thank you to all who volunteered to edit stories and provide feedback for our authors: Aubrey Yeh, Carla Meyrink, Casey Korder, Heather Green, Karie Frauenhoffer, Mary-Lou Dunnigan, Meagan Kelly, Michelle Joyce, Nick Brierley, Rebecca Jackson, and Sarah Joncas.

A huge round of applause and hugs for all 53 authors! Thank you for taking the time to share your stories. I know just how difficult it was to think of the story you wanted to tell, write it, and comb through feedback. You all are amazing teachers and leaders.

Thank you to my boyfriend Jonathan, for being my comic relief and reminding me not to take life so seriously.

Lastly, I must thank my dog, Ollie. He helped me with every stage of this project--although usually him "helping" meant bringing me a toy right when I was in the middle of something.

These are my thank-yous. Now it's your turn.

Go thank a teacher who impacted you, went above and beyond for you, or made a difference in your life. Send them an email, a text, a postcard, an owl...whatever you have to do. Please, take a moment to acknowledge their love and hard work.

About the Editor

Mari Venturino is a 7th grade science and AVID teacher and Blended Learning Specialist in San Diego, CA. She is a Google For Education Certified Trainer and Innovator, and is Leading Edge Certified in Online and Blended Instruction. Mari was awarded CUE Outstanding Emerging Teacher of the Year and ISTE Emerging Leader in 2017.

When she's not teaching, she enjoys reading, cooking, and playing with her dog Ollie.

Find Mari on Twitter (@MsVenturino) or on her blog (blog.mariventurino.com).

46628058R00157

Made in the USA
Middletown, DE
05 August 2017